MEL THOMPSON

Leading THE *Way*

VOLUME 2

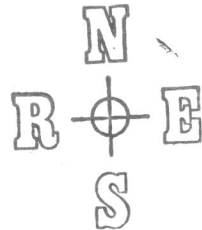

N
R E
S

Hodder & Stoughton
LONDON SYDNEY AUCKLAND TORONTO

Acknowledgements

The Publishers would like to thank the following for permission to reproduce material in this volume:

Amnesty International; Grafton Books for the extracts from *From Beirut To Jerusalem* by Dr Swee Chai Ang (1989); Hodder and Stoughton Ltd for the extracts from *Tutu: Voice of the Voiceless* by Shirley du Boulay (1988); Jackie Pullinger for the quotation from *The Law of Love*, a Contracts International presentation, written and directed by Penelope Lee; Sidgwick and Jackson Ltd for the extracts from *Is That It?* by Bob Geldof; The South African Council of Churches for the quotation from *This We Can Do For Justice and Peace*; Ateliers et Presses de Taizé for the extracts from a Taizé publication, © Ateliers et presses de Taizé, F-71250 Taizé communauté.

The publishers would also like to thank the following for their permission to reproduce copyright photographs in this book:

Sudarshan Abrol/Mayfield School – pp32, 34, 35; Amnesty International – pp22, 26, 27; Band Aid – p45; CND – pp66, 71, 73; Daily Express – pp40, 4; Daily Telegraph – p55; Nick Danziger – pp76, 77; Format Partners – p27; FWBO – pp58, 60, 62, 63; Judy Goldhill – p14; Robert Harding Picture Library – p85; Jewish Chronicle – p16; London Features – p41; Lesley MacIntyre – p72; Presses d Taizé – pp84, 89, 90, 91; Swee Chai Ang – pp48, 5 56; Mel Thompson – pp87, 88; Topham Picture Source – pp4, 5, 7, 8, 10, 12, 18, 42, 46, 68, 69, 78, 81.

Every effort has been made to trace and acknowledge ownership of copyright. The publishers will be glad to make suitable arrangements with any copyright holders whom it has not been possible to contact.

British Library Cataloguing in Publication Data
Thompson, M. R. (Melvyn Rodney) 1946–
Leading the way
1. Social problems. Christian viewpoints
I. Title
261.83

ISBN 0–340–51955–X Vol. 1
ISBN 0–340–52347–6 Vol. 2

ISBN 0 340 52347 6

First published 1991

© 1991 Mel Thompson

Typeset by Gecko Ltd, Bicester
Printed in Great Britain for the educational publishing division of Hodder and Stoughton Ltd, Mill Road, Dunton Green, Sevenoaks, Kent by Thomson Litho Ltd, East Kilbride

Contents

Introduction

Leading the Way looks at personal, social and religious issues through the eyes of those who are involved in them. Each chapter features someone whose beliefs and convictions about life have led him or her to a commitment to help others – by doing something practical for those in need, by raising money or working for charities, or by promoting their religious beliefs. They give their own comments, showing what is most important for them, and how they came to be involved.

Some of the people in this book are well known, others are not; some have started new organisations, others work within those started by other people; but they are all equally *leading the way*. For each of them, their life and work has been changed because of something about which they feel strongly. *Leading the way* is not reserved for the famous, it is for everyone.

To the teacher

The chapters in *Leading the Way* have been compiled from interviews with, or material published by, the people featured. Each chapter therefore represents a personal statement, rather than an objective assessment, although some background information has been included in order to help pupils to understand the issues with which these people are concerned. The book is intended to be a basis for further reflection and discussion, as well as an introduction to some of the most important personal, social and religious issues of our day.

Implicit in the chapters – and drawn out in some of the 'Over to you' assignments – is the idea of *leading the way*. All the people featured have found that their way of life has been challenged and changed by responding to some practical, moral or religious conviction. Some are leading a way of life very different from that which they imagined when they were younger. Some have led the way by setting up new organisations or ventures. Others have become spokespersons for great issues. Not all of them are well known – which may serve to show pupils that they too may be challenged to 'lead the way'.

All the major world religions have the idea of 'the way' that people are to follow – a way based on moral and religious convictions, in contrast to a life of aimless drifting. Some of those featured in *Leading the Way* speak about their religious beliefs, others do not, but all illustrate a sense of purpose and direction in life – a direction which provides the context within which religious and moral ideas make sense, and which can show their relevance.

Desmond Tutu

CAMPAIGNING AGAINST APARTHEID

Desmond Tutu is the Archbishop of Cape Town, leader of the Anglican Church in Southern Africa. He believes that, as a Christian, he has a duty to seek justice and peace for all the people of South Africa, whatever the colour of their skin. He is a leading opponent of apartheid – the political system that separates people of different races in South Africa – on the grounds that it denies to many black people their basic human rights. He wants South Africa to change, and to allow greater sharing between people of different races, but he opposes violence as a means to bring that change about. Although involved in political issues, Desmond Tutu does not see himself as a politician, but as a religious leader, concerned first and foremost to follow the teaching of Christ.

Desmond Tutu was born in South Africa, in the town of Klerksdorp in Western Transvaal, on 7 October 1939. His father was headteacher at the Methodist primary school there, but, like most black South Africans, his family was poor.

He was a hard-working boy, and quick to learn. At the age of fourteen he went to Western High School, which was for black children only. It was crowded there, with up to sixty children in a class. As a child, Desmond learned what it was like to be poor, and to see white children who had more money, better homes to live in, and better schools to go to.

Soon after starting at the High School, Desmond was ill with tuberculosis, a disease which affects the lungs, and he had to spend twenty months in hospital. While he was there he did a lot of reading, and was visited regularly by Father Trevor Huddleston, a priest from the Community of the Resurrection. This was the Christian community in whose hostel Desmond had been staying while at school.

> *If we do not share more equitably, then those who have so much are in danger of losing it all.*

Being in hospital gave him time to think about his life, and he became more serious about his Christian religion. After leaving hospital, he started helping with services at the parish church of St Paul in Munsieville, where he lived with his family. He travelled to school from there, and worked late at night to finish his studies.

It was while Desmond Tutu was at school that, in 1948, the National Party came to power in South Africa. They promised apartheid (which means 'apartness'). Black, white, Indian and coloured people were to live and develop separately. They were to have different areas in which to live, and were not allowed to marry people of a different colour. Everyone had to be registered according to the colour of his or her skin. Black and white people had been kept apart and had led very different lives before 1948, but apartheid was seen as a form of government which made sure that the white people could continue to live in comfort, and that the black majority had no chance of gaining power in South Africa.

At first, Desmond Tutu decided that he wanted to be a doctor. He gained a place at medical school, but there was no money to pay for his training. So instead of this, he studied to be a teacher. In 1954 he gained his certificate and started teaching at his old school. But, as one of the few black Africans qualified to go to university, he was determined to improve his education, so he worked for a

He was ordained in 1960, the same year that many black people were killed by troops at Sharpeville, while demonstrating against the pass-laws (by which every black person had to carry a 'pass' in order to be allowed into a white area). He had to ask himself what it meant to be a Christian leader in a country where there was such violence and injustice.

postal degree from the University of South Africa in his spare time.

He married in 1955. With his wife Leah he settled in Munsieville, and he taught at the high school, which was next to the Anglican primary school where his father was the headteacher.

Although Desmond Tutu enjoyed his work, the government imposed rules to limit what could be taught to black children, and after three years he felt that he could not continue as a teacher. He had already been helping with church services, and he was accepted for training as a priest.

After two years, Desmond Tutu went to England in order to study at King's College, London. He wanted to be as well qualified as possible, determined that, when he returned to South Africa, there would be no excuse for anyone to say that he was not as well trained as a white priest would be.

Desmond Tutu and his family then returned to South Africa, where he taught in a college and was Anglican chaplain to a university. Later he taught in Lesotho, a small mountainous country. Then, in 1972, he again went to England, this time to work for an organisation which gave grants for education. He was responsible for the money which was sent to Africa.

In 1975 he returned to South Africa to become Dean of Johannesburg, which meant that he would be in charge of running the cathedral there. Although he and Leah had friends in England, and their children were at school there, he felt that it was right for him to go back to South Africa. It was the first time that a black priest had been given such an important position in the Church, and he hoped that it would encourage others.

It was a time of unrest in the townships, and Desmond Tutu wrote to John Vorster, the Prime Minister, appealing to him to help the situation. The cathedral was racially mixed, and Desmond Tutu saw it as an image of what South Africa could become if all the people lived and worked together.

Shortly after becoming Dean, he accepted the invitation to become Bishop of Lesotho, the small country in which he had taught a few years before. After a year there, he returned to South Africa in order to become General Secretary to the South African Council of Churches. The council had declared that apartheid was against the Gospel

66 *The Bible is the most revolutionary, the most radical book there is.* 99

If he had moved into the official house offered to the Dean, he would have lived as an 'honorary white' in a white area. Instead, he and his family chose to live in Soweto, a township of more than a million black people, 12 miles from Johannesburg. In contrast to the white areas, few houses in Soweto had electricity, and there were no properly made-up roads.

of Jesus Christ, and, as its leader, Desmond Tutu was able to speak out against the injustices that the black people of South Africa were suffering. He insisted that his work was not political, but that he was simply following the teachings of Christ.

In 1984 he was awarded the Nobel Peace Prize for his work to promote the human dignity of all the people of South Africa. People all over the world were keen to hear what he had to say, and he became a respresentative of all who were working for justice and peaceful change in South Africa.

The following year, he became Bishop of Johannesburg, and in 1986 he was enthroned as Archbishop of Cape Town, the most senior position in the Anglican Church in South Africa.

66 *When God encounters injustice, oppression, exploitation, he takes sides. Then God and the Bible are subversive of such a situation.*

Our God is not God who sanctifies the status quo. He is a God of surprises, uprooting the powerful and the unjust to establish his Kingdom. 99

Desmond Tutu receives the Nobel Peace Prize from the chairman of the Nobel Committee.

As Archbishop, Desmond Tutu heads a Church which includes people of all races. He is concerned that black and white should work together in peace, and that the Church should give a lead, showing what is possible in South Africa. He is against violence, although he can understand why some people are driven to it when all other means of gaining freedom seem to fail. He often travels across the world, speaking about the situation in South Africa, and campaigning on behalf of those who are oppressed, wherever they are.

A demonstration against
Apartheid in 1989. Anger
and frustration can easily
lead to violence.

Apartheid

66 *We have to try as
the Church to help the
people in their
immediate need, but that
is just short term. I
think the long-term
strategy of the churches
is to continue to be a
conscience of the
community, pointing
out how horrendous this
system is, and how
inconsistent with the
Gospel of Jesus Christ it
must be.* **99**

Apartheid is the name given to the South African policy of
'separate development'. It means that people of different
races in South Africa – black, white, coloured and Indian –
have their own areas in which to live, their own schools
and universities, their own 'homelands'. Those who
support apartheid argue that each people has its own way
of life and its own values. In practice, however, apartheid
has been a means of allowing a minority of white people to
control the government of South Africa, preventing people
of the other races from owning the best land or enjoying
the many benefits of South Africa's wealth.

In 1951 the government set up the Bantustans (*Bantu* is
the African word for 'people'). These are ten homelands, to
which the black South African people were told they
belonged. Although 73 per cent of the population were
black, they got only 13 per cent of the land, much of which
was the poorest land in South Africa. If the government
decides that an area should be used by whites only, the
black people who live there may be forcibly removed from
their homes, which are then demolished, and are taken to
resettlement camps. They are told that they are not citizens
of South Africa, but of one of the 'homelands'. They may
go back to their old home village only as foreigners, in
order to work there. They have no rights there, even if
their families have lived in that place for many generations.

Because there is little work in the 'homelands', many men work in the white areas of South Africa, living in single-sex hostels and visiting their families perhaps only once a year. Desmond Tutu and others argue that this leads to the break-up of family life.

This is a resettlement camp. Black people have been taken from their homes in white areas and dumped here.

Your mother is a widow. Does she get a grant or a pension?

No.

What do you do for food?

We borrow food.

Have you returned any of your food?

No.

What do you do when you cannot borrow food?

We drink water to fill our stomachs.

More than three million people have been uprooted from their homes and live in terrible conditions. Yet they are all created in the image of God! They are all starving here because of a deliberate policy of forced population removals.

In South Africa it is not a matter of civil rights, it is a question of fundamental human rights – the recognition that a black person is a human being, created in the image of God.

Although some black people hold responsible positions, and a few are able to earn a good living, most remain poor. They may be no worse off in terms of money and food than some other people in Africa, but they see all around them the wealth that their work has helped to create, and yet they cannot share in it. This reminds them of the unfairness of their society every day. They love the land and feel that they belong to it, but they are told that they have no rights there, and that they are citizens of a 'homeland' that they may never have seen, far away from where they live.

Around large cities in South Africa are 'townships', where black workers live. Getting up early in the morning, these people have to travel into the wealthy suburbs to work for white families, or into the city centre.

Life in the townships can become violent. People become angry because they can see no way to change the way they are forced to live. The authorities can arrest people and put them in prison without trial, they can use force if people do not obey them, and they can prevent press photographers from reporting what is happening. All these things only make the people who live in the townships more angry.

Many white people in South Africa have never been into a township, and don't know what it is like to live there. They have never seen the homelands from which the migrant workers come. They may be happy to have black people cooking their food and looking after their children, but they do not want to know what life is like for them once they return to their homes.

Because of their frustration and anger at apartheid, there is also violence in South Africa between black people, especially if some are thought to be helping the government. This is what happened at a funeral in 1985.

Four young men have died in an explosion. I must go and speak to the crowd of mourners at their funeral.

Don't use violence. We must change apartheid by peaceful means!

He's a spy!

Let the dog die!

Why don't you use methods of which we will be proud when we become free? This violence undermines the struggle!

No, it encourages the struggle!

Why don't you allow us to deal with them as they treat us?

"No-one should kill—even if provoked."

If this violence continues, I will pack my bags, collect my family and leave this beautiful country that I love so passionately.

But Desmond Tutu stayed, and continues to work for peaceful change in South Africa.

11

The South African government hopes that, by gradually doing away with apartheid, and by giving them increasing political power, the black, coloured and Asian people will be content, and will hope to benefit gradually from South Africa's wealth.

During 1990 the pace of change in South Africa increased. Nelson Mandela, an important black political leader, was released from prison, the government agreed to work towards dismantling the system of apartheid, and the African National Congress (a major political group campaigning against apartheid) agreed to give up its policy of using force as a means of trying to bring about change.

Nelson Mandela waves to supporters in Cape Town in February 1990. This was his first public speech after spending 27 years in jail.

66 *Freedom has to be shared, otherwise those who have it have no time to enjoy their separate freedoms – they are too busy guarding it with guns and guard dogs and states of emergency. We all share in each other's glory – and equally in each other's shame.* 99

Some black leaders have argued that the white minority will never give up control of the country, and that in the future the black majority will claim its fair share of the wealth by force. People who think like this, and who are frustrated by the slowness of change in South Africa, tend also to attack those within the black community who try to work alongside the whites by taking the limited powers that they are allowed within the townships. There is also great resentment of anyone thought to be a spy on behalf of the police, as the story earlier in this chapter shows.

Desmond Tutu fears that the struggle for justice in South Africa may end in violence, but he wants to do all in his power to bring about change by peaceful means. He believes that this is the right attitude for a Christian to take when faced with cruelty and oppression.

Desmond Tutu is *leading the way* towards justice, peace and understanding between all the people of South Africa. He believes that this is something he must do in response to the Gospel of Jesus Christ, and the Christian belief that all people are made in the image of God, no matter what the colour of their skin.

Over to you

1 Under a system of apartheid, the most important thing to know about a person is the colour of his or her skin.
   ● Write down a list of all the things that you would want to say about yourself if you were introducing yourself to a stranger.
   ● Which of these things do you think is the most important for the stranger to know?
   ● Which of these things can you have in common with someone who has skin of a different colour from yours?

2 Where do you feel most at home? Have you lived in your present house for very long? Do you feel that you really belong there? Now imagine that you are told that you can't stay in the place that you call home – that you are really a citizen of a faraway country and that you should move there. Would you be prepared to go?

3 From what you have read in this chapter, do you think that Desmond Tutu and those who think like him will succeed in bringing about change through peaceful means, or do you think that there will be civil war in South Africa? Do you agree with those who think that it is right to use violence to bring about a change?

4 In South Africa, the political situation is changing all the time. This chapter was written in 1989, and reflects the situation up to that date. If you are doing a project or an assessment on apartheid, you might want to collect cuttings from newspapers showing up-to-date events, and then ask yourself if these are things that Desmond Tutu would or would not support, based on what you know of his views from this chapter.

For more information on the life and work of Desmond Tutu, see Shirley Du Boulay, *Tutu: Voice of the Voiceless* (Hodder & Stoughton, 1988) and Naomi Tutu *Words of Desmond Tutu* (Hodder & Stoughton 1989).

Julia Neuberger

LOOKING AT QUESTIONS OF MORALITY, FROM EMBRYO TO ADULT

Julia Neuberger is a rabbi in the non-Orthodox (or Liberal) tradition of Judaism. She points out that the place of women in the Jewish community is changing fast, and that it is important to have both men and women rabbis available for the personal support and guidance of people in synagogue congregations. She is concerned with the way in which people come to decisions about what is morally right, and is particularly involved with questions about research on human embryos. She has also been working to establish a hospice for people from all faiths who are coming towards the end of their lives. She leads the way in attacking what she sees as nonsense and bigotry, and tries to replace them with common sense and sympathy in dealing with the important questions about how people should treat one another.

> 66 *I want to make people stop and think, and not just have gut reactions to moral issues. I want them to look at what really is morally right in the area of freedom and justice.* 99

Although Julia Neuberger was brought up in a Jewish family, and went to synagogue fairly regularly as a child, she did not set out to become a rabbi. Her first ambition was to be an archaeologist.

She was particularly interested in the remains of the ancient civilisations of the Near East, and went to Cambridge University in 1969 to read Assyriology. This is the study of the Assyrians, whose empires were based in the area of what is modern Iraq from about 1900 BCE until 600 BCE. As part of her course, she was expected to visit archaeological sites in the Near East, but she was refused entry to Iraq in 1969 because she was Jewish (Iraq, being an Arab country, regarded all Jews as supporting Israel, and this was a time of tension between Israel and its Arab neighbours). The following year she was refused entry into

> 66 *It was while I was doing Hebrew at Cambridge that I first had the idea that I would like to be a rabbi.* 99

> 66 *At first, my family thought it was a bit weird, then not too bad – but they've been quite supportive.* 99

> 66 *The reactions of my male colleagues at college were mixed, but it didn't really trouble me. I was used to being in a minority group at Cambridge – where men outnumbered women by ten to one – and I'm quite tough!* 99

Turkey because she was British. The opportunities for following her chosen career were blocked.

While doing Assyriology, Julia Neuberger had studied Hebrew. This was an easy option for her because she already knew some Hebrew through her religion. Now that a career in Assyrian archaeology was no longer possible, she changed to Hebrew as the main subject for her degree.

The idea that she should become a rabbi was suggested to her by one of her teachers at Cambridge. At that time there were no women rabbis at all in Britain (although one other woman had already started training to become one), so the idea must have come as quite a surprise to her family and friends. Orthodox Jews do not accept women as rabbis, and among Reform Jews many synagogues prefer to have men, so there are still very few women rabbis.

After Cambridge, Julia Neuberger went to Leo Baeck College, where rabbis of the non-Orthodox (Liberal, Reform and Conservative) tradition are trained. The course at Leo Baeck College normally lasts five years, but she was able to do it in four because she had already studied Hebrew at Cambridge. When she arrived, she wasn't the only woman there, for Jackie Tabick (who was to become Britain's first woman rabbi) was already two years ahead of her on the course. But not all of the men who were training with them approved of women becoming rabbis. Some did not really think that women were equal, or that they should be in charge of the congregation at a synagogue. In spite of this, Julia Neuberger enjoyed her time at college, and especially the practical experience of going out and working among synagogue congregations.

Women in the ministry

The place of women in society has changed a great deal in recent years, and this affects people of every religious group. At one time it was expected that a Jewish woman would spend most of her time at home, being a wife and a mother. That is no longer true. More Jewish women today – from both the Orthodox and the Liberal and Reform traditions – are following careers outside the home.

Women also seek to take a lead in organised religion, and
in Judaism there is a small but growing number of women
rabbis.

Although there is opposition to the idea that women
should become rabbis, once a rabbi has actually been
appointed to a congregation she is accepted by those
people. This is because they have taken the decision that
they are going to have a woman as their rabbi, and once
that have done that, they are bound to support her.

Do women have a special contribution to make, when it
comes to the practical side of helping people in
congregations? Julia Neuberger thinks that there are things
that women can do that men can't – but it's not simply a
matter of saying that women can do this and men can do
that. It depends on the individuals.

Of course, some rabbis work full time as teachers – but
among those who are in pastoral work (that is, working to
help people with their personal and spiritual needs), Julia
Neuberger thinks that it is important to have both men and
women available.

She believes that young women are often more naturally
religious than young men, and that girls have a strong
spiritual side to their nature. Although there are very

Rabbi Julia Neuberger leading
worship in a synagogue.

religious men, they tend to develop their religious sensitivity later in life. As a general rule, however, she does not think that women are more religious than men.

She sees Judaism as a religion which has been rather dominated by men – especially in Orthodox Jewish communities. Much of the activity in which men are involved has to do with the organisation of the religion; it is public and visible. It is therefore difficult to tell from this how deeply religious all this activity is. Some people argue that it does not matter that women do not take much part in the public organisation of Orthodox Jewish communities because they have a strong, private spiritual life instead. Although Julia Neuberger agrees that some women do have this spiritual life, she is not sure that this is a good reason for them to take little part in the public side of their religion.

66 *There is evidence to show that girls between the ages of thirteen and sixteen go through a deeply religious phase.* **99**

Medical ethics

When doctors and nurses want to test out some new form of treatment, they may need to carry out experiments which involve human beings. An example of this is the way in which a new drug is tested on patients (with their permission). People who agree to take part in a test are divided into two groups – half of them have the new drug, and half are given what looks like a drug, but which does nothing at all. This second group is called the 'control group' – and by comparing the differences between them and the group who have had the real drug, researchers are able to tell if the drug is actually helping. Is this fair on the control group of patients? Should people be told if they are having the real drug or the dummy one?

This is just one very simple example of the way in which doing medical research can involve moral questions about how people should be treated. The rules for carrying out medical research are often guided by committees of people who discuss the ethics (morality) of this. Julia Neuberger is working on a research project for the King's Fund Institute. She is looking at the way in which these research ethics committees work in Britain, and who serves on them. She is therefore involved with a whole range of questions to do with 'medical ethics', and she makes her views known by writing on these topics in newspapers.

When issues concerning medical ethics affect people personally, feelings run high. This demonstration was against proposed changes to the Embryology bill in April 1990, which was to further limit the period during which women could have abortions.

❝ *We need to find out what the possible benefits are of embryo research, how likely they are to be reached.* **❞**

Embryo research

Julia Neuberger is a member of the Interim Licensing Authority, which has been set up to decide who should be allowed to carry out research on human embryos – the very early stage after conception, in what may grow to become a human baby – and to look at problems of artificial methods of human fertilisation.

She is not unsympathetic to embryo research, but opposes some of the arguments that are used for doing it. In particular, she is not yet convinced that some of the work cannot be done by what is known as 'genetic engineering' (working with the genes which tell every cell of the body how it should develop), rather than using human embryos.

There is also debate about the point at which to stop research – when does the tiny bundle of cells actually start to become a human being? She does not agree with the view (held by Catholics and others) which says that it is absolutely wrong to do embryo research in all circumstances – that the embryo has a soul and becomes a unique human being from the moment of conception, and therefore cannot be touched.

DAY 1

DAY 10

DAY 15

32 mm

DAY 21

WEEK 24

Unlike this foetus, the human embryo is very small in the first days after conception.

66 *Judaism is very life affirming, and very family affirming – so the idea of assisted conception is viewed on the whole quite positively.* 99

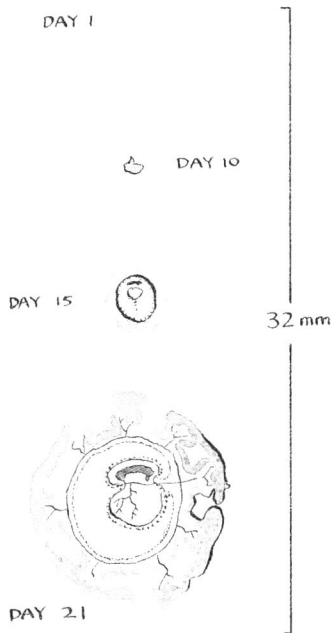

Others argue that, during the first fourteen days, the embryo is no more than a bundle of cells, and that it has not developed to the point where it becomes a separate living being. They therefore agree with the idea that research can be done using embryos up to that age.

It is hoped that research on embryos will enable doctors to understand more about some serious defects – such as Down's syndrome, muscular dystrophy and cystic fibrosis – with which some people are born, and which develop in the embryo stage.

Julia Neuberger is totally in favour of artificial fertilisation techniques (ways in which a man and woman can be artificially helped to conceive a child, when it is not possible for them to do so naturally), including the ones that some people object to, like surrogacy. Surrogacy is the technique in which a 'surrogate' or substitute mother agrees to have a fertilised embryo implanted in her womb, so that she can give birth to a baby on behalf of the woman who is unable to have a natural pregnancy.

It is argued that more research on embryos is needed in order to make these artificial techniques more successful, enabling childless couples to have a family of their own.

When a human egg is fertilised, it is less than one tenth of a millimetre in diameter. It divides into two cells, then into four and so on. When this bundle of cells is about fourteen days old, it should become embedded in the womb, ready to develop into a baby. Until that stage, it is not possible yet to tell if the cells are going to develop into a single child or twins, or if they are going to be successful in becoming implanted at all. Most fertilised eggs do not succeed in becoming babies. From fourteen days, the embryo has a primitive heart, and is about one millimetre long.

When human eggs are fertilised artificially, relatively few of them are found to be suitable for implanting into a womb. The majority will be wasted – just as happens naturally in the human body. Part of the debate about embryo research is whether or not it is right for these 'spare' embryos to be used in experiments.

The reaction of the Jewish community to these issues is mixed. Some of the more conservative Orthodox thinkers opppose these techniques, but others are more sympathetic, and some Orthodox Jews are directly involved with this work.

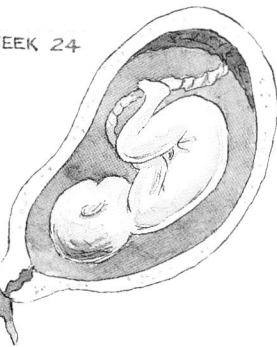

Care of the dying

Julia Neuberger has been involved in setting up an inter-faith hospice in North London. A hospice is a place where those who are coming to the end of their lives can receive special medical and nursing care. She thinks that it is important to recognise the special needs of members of religions other than Christianity, and to provide for them both practically and spiritually.

People simply don't want to die – and yet they have to face the prospect of putting their personal affairs in order, and accepting that they are at the end of their lives. Some people get angry when they realise that they are dying, and feel that life has been unfair to them!

If you feel angry, but don't tell anyone about it, it can make you feel tense and miserable. It is as if your anger were turned in on yourself. The more you can express your anger, and tell other people how you feel, the easier it is to cope with that anger and do something practical to help.

Julia Neuberger finds that, once people are able to express their feelings of anger, they can feel more settled and are better able to sort out what needs to be done in a very practical way. Judaism affirms the value of family life, and many of the problems faced by Jewish people who are dying are about making arrangements to see that members of their family are taken care of once they are no longer with them.

> 66 *Judaism is so life affirming that people find it hard to accept that they are dying, unless they are over ninety! They get angry!* 99

> 66 *We live in a society which looks for instant gratification – everything provided, and all problems solved, with no effort. We need to get beyond this, and make people think about what is right.* 99

Getting rid of nonsense!

In her work, Julia Neuberger is concerned to cut through what she sees as nonsense in the way that some people in positions of authority argue – and to look for what really is morally right. She is concerned about relationships between human beings – whether they are sexual, or business, or family relationships – and the whole way in which individuals are treated in society. She feels that the media can contribute a great deal by making people aware of the issues, forcing them to stop and think.

Julia Neuberger *leads the way* in discussing moral issues through her writing and her involvement in the world of medical research.

Over to you

1 Do you think that women have special qualities to offer when they work as ministers of religion? Are these *only* found in women, or can men share them as well?
   - Try to find more information about women ministers of religion (perhaps from newspaper articles about Christian women who want to become priests, or about women rabbis). List the arguments that are used for and against having women as ministers, and add your own comments.
   - Imagine you are a woman, qualified as a rabbi or Christian minister. You are being interviewed by representatives of a synagogue (or a church), some of whom are against having a woman to minister to them. Join with other students to act out the possible interview, or write down the points you would want to make.

2 Doctors and nurses should always do what is best for their patients. Researchers need to find out all they can about new forms of treatment. Suppose that a new drug – never before tested on humans – is to start its clinical trials. Nobody knows if it will work – if it will help cure the patients, or make them worse. Working as a group, discuss and write down the rules that you would want to give to the medical researchers (e.g. should the patients be told about the trial? should they be told all the possible dangers? should there be a 'control group', and what, if anything, should they be told? should you continue with the drug, even if a patient seems to be getting worse?).

3 In nature, not all fertilised eggs (whether human or of other creatures) are able to implant and develop into a baby, yet each has the *potential* to do so. A great deal of potential life is therefore wasted.
   - List some of the possible benefits of embryo research.
   - List possible objections to experimenting with embryos that might have the potential for becoming babies.
   - From the above lists, draw up your conclusions about whether it is morally right to carry out embryo research. (You will need to say something about when you believe a new individual human being is created – at conception, or some time later?)

Dan Jones

CAMPAIGNING FOR PRISONERS OF CONSCIENCE

Dan Jones is Head of the Campaigns Department at Amnesty International's British headquarters in London. Amnesty International is an organisation which seeks to help all those who have been put in prison, not because they have committed a crime, but simply on account of their political or religious views, or because of their colour or race. Amnesty also works to oppose torture and execution. Dan Jones is part of a team which receives news about people from all round the world whose human rights have been abused in this way. He passes on this information to groups of Amnesty supporters in Britain, helping them to campaign effectively for the release of those who are suffering unfairly.

Dan Jones was born in the Lake District during the Second World War, and moved home several times before settling in London. His original ambition, while at school, was to become an entomologist – someone who studies insects. In fact, he started his career as a teacher in Brighton, and while he was there he started to do community work, becoming involved with young people and their emotional problems.

Then he spent twenty years as a youth and community worker in the East End of London, where he was particularly involved with young people from Asian families. His first contacts with Amnesty came when he was involved with trade union work and was asked to support fellow trade unionists in Chile and South America, and later when he needed information to help an Iranian student who was going to be deported from Britain.

In the early 1980s he set up an Amnesty letter-writing group, and helped to organise public meetings about human rights. He was already an experienced campaigner when he took the opportunity to join the organisation full time to help organise its campaigns in Britain.

Amnesty International

All human beings are born free and equal in dignity and rights. They are endowed with reason and conscience and should act towards one another in a spirit of brotherhood.

From the Universal Declaration of Human Rights

In 1961, a British lawyer called Peter Benenson wrote a newspaper article entitled 'The Forgotten Prisoners'. It asked people to work for the release of those who were in prison because of their political or religious beliefs, and was published worldwide. As a result, more than one thousand people wrote back to him, offering support for the idea that there should be an organisation to help prisoners of conscience – Amnesty International was started.

It is now one of the world's largest international voluntary organisations – with more than 700,000 members and subscribers in over 150 countries. There are 'national sections' of Amnesty in 46 countries, and more than 4,000 local groups in Africa, Asia, Europe, the Americas and the Middle East.

Amnesty International is independent of any government, or political or religious group, and is concerned for those who suffer abuse, whoever they are, and whatever their views. It does not ask for, or receive, money from governments, but depends on donations given by individual supporters. Amnesty works to do three things:

66 *Human rights are everybody's business. We are here to let people know about abuses of human rights all over the world, and to tell them what they can do to help.* 99

1 It seeks the release of *prisoners of conscience*. These are people detained because of their beliefs, colour, sex, ethnic origin, language or religion, who have not used or encouraged others to use violence.

2 It works for *fair and prompt trials* for all political prisoners, and on behalf of such people detained without charge or trial.

3 It opposes the *death penalty* and *torture*, or other cruel, inhuman or degrading treatment of prisoners.

Some people have been put in prison because they have questioned what their government is doing; others may have been arrested while on a demonstration, or for belonging to a religious, political or trade union group that their government has banned. Some have refused to do military service, on grounds that it goes against their beliefs. A 'prisoner of conscience' is therefore someone who has been arrested for nothing more than claiming what should be his or her 'rights' as a human being.

Since it started, Amnesty International has adopted or investigated more than 32,000 cases of prisoners of conscience. At any one time, it will be involved with about 4,000 of them worldwide. Amnesty also investigates and publishes reports on human rights violations. It sends representatives to countries where there are prisoners of conscience, to speak to people in the government, to appear at trials, and to carry out on-the-spot investigations.

Almost half the countries in the world hold people in prison because of their beliefs of one sort or another. In one-third of countries, there is evidence that prisoners are tortured.

The International Secretariat

It is important to have accurate information. This is the job of the International Secretariat (based in London) – a research department employing 240 people. It collects information about human rights abuses from journalists, newspapers and magazines, radio and television broadcasts, lawyers, priests and opposition groups, and even from government sources. It also receives letters from prisoners themselves, and from their families, explaining what has happened to them. To make sure that the evidence is examined fairly, those who work as researchers for Amnesty are not allowed to consider cases of people in their own country of origin. (People from forty different nationalities work in Amnesty's research department.)

Many political prisoners are held in jail without any charge. Amnesty may ask for a trial to be held, so that the guilt or innocence of the person can be decided. Only when it is satisfied that this is genuinely a prisoner of conscience will Amnesty campaign for the person's release, and argue that he or she should not have been put in prison in the first place.

Amnesty insists that the people it adopts as 'prisoners of conscience' should not have advocated violence, but it makes its own judgement about this, and does not necessarily reject the call to help a prisoner just because a government has accused him or her of supporting an organisation that is violent.

What does Amnesty do to help?

Each of Amnesty's prisoners of conscience is 'adopted' by one of Amnesty's 300 local groups. About 10,000 people in Britain belong to these groups.

Members of the group appeal to the government of the country where the prisoner is held, to newspapers, and to anyone else in authority who might be able to help. They may get up a petition, or stage some sort of demonstration on behalf of the prisoner. They may need to argue that the prisoner should be charged and given a proper trial. If the person has already been tried and found guilty, Amnesty may still support him or her as a prisoner of conscience if it believes that the law under which he or she has been sentenced is itself a violation of international human rights.

As well as campaigning for the release of prisoners of conscience, Amnesty also has funds to give relief to prisoners and to their families – this may mean that a prisoner can receive blankets and winter clothes, or his or her family may get money for food, for schooling or for the cost of prison visits. It may also give help to pay for medical treatment for those who have been tortured.

Members of Amnesty do not campaign on behalf of prisoners in their own country. This helps to prevent anyone complaining that people campaign in order to help their own political group. Amnesty members' concern is simply for the prisoner, not for any political organisation. For the same reason, Amnesty groups are not allowed to support prisoners in countries which are in conflict with the groups' country. Over a period of time, each group is given a number of prisoners to help, and these are chosen so that they come from different parts of the world and hold different political views.

Amnesty often criticises the way governments treat their own citizens, but it is not always governments that are to blame. Amnesty also condemns any use of torture or execution by groups opposed to a government. Amnesty is not automatically against violence, and it does not judge whether a violent struggle is right or wrong.

66 Things are changing fast; all our information has to be bang up to date. 99

66 They write to the prisoner and his or her family, giving support and encouragement. 99

66 It may be someone whose ideas you disagree with from first to last – but I still support his or her right to speak out freely, and to be treated properly as a human being. 99

In each issue of *Amnesty!*, the organisation's bi-monthly journal, there are six 'prisoners of the month' whose cases are particularly serious. Readers are asked to write in support of them, and are told the address to which their letters of appeal should be sent. Many of Amnesty's 60,000 supporters in Britain do not belong to local groups, but help in this way.

Governments often hope that nobody will notice, and that the rest of the world will quietly forget someone whom it keeps in prison, or intends to execute. By making the facts public, and by launching campaigns, Amnesty shows governments around the world that they cannot get away with this.

Here are two examples: —

Erick ROMERO CANALES, El Salvador

A student, Erick Romero Canales is one of hundreds of people who have "disappeared" after being taken into military custody in El Salvador.

Erick Romero Canales is a seventeen year old student from Apopa, San Salvador.

Shortly after leaving his home on 18 November 1989 Erick Romero Canales was detained in front of several witnesses by uniformed soldiers of the First Infantry Brigade.

He was kept at a military post two blocks from his home, where his mother was allowed to visit him and bring him food. A First Brigade lieutenant at the military post reportedly told Mrs Canales that he had been ordered to capture her son because he had been accused of being a member of the armed opposition group, the Farabundo Marti National Liberation Front.

The next morning his mother watched Erick Canales being taken away by First Brigade soldiers in an army jeep, blindfolded and with his hands tied. She has not seen him since.

Mrs Canales has tried to find her son. She began by making enquiries at the First Brigade Headquarters and police headquarters around the capital. All denied holding him. According to her, ten days later the First Brigade lieutenant who had arrested Erick Romero told her that he had been ordered by a superior officer to kill her son, but he said that he had told the officer to "give the boy a chance, because we don't know whether he is [a guerilla] or not".

Despite the presentation of a habeas corpus writ and constant enquiries to the military and judiciary by human rights organisations, his whereabouts are still unknown. One military official told Mrs Canales that she would be killed if she continued to make accusations. But Mrs Canales will continue her search: "I just want to know where he is, so that I can be at peace", she says.

These events are part of a continuing pattern of unacknowledged detentions and "disappearances" in El Salvador. Numerous trade unionists, cooperative workers and youths are reported to have gone missing following their detention by members of the security forces since November 1989, when the conflict and the FMLN intensified dramatically. Little has been done by the current administration to investigate and clarify the fate of hundreds of Salvadorians who have "disappeared" in recent years, under this and previous governments.

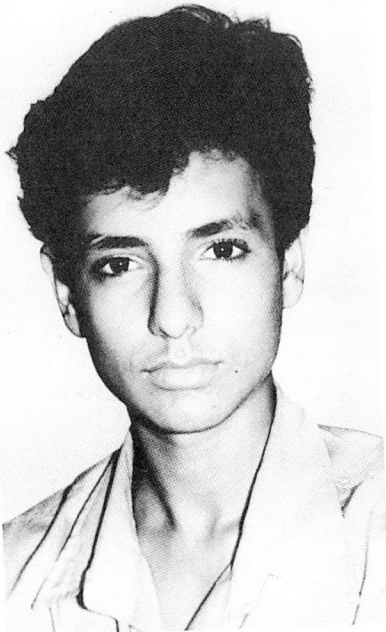

<u>Jack MAPANJE, Malawi</u>

Malawian poet Jack Mapanje was arrested in 1987. Three years later he is still being detained without charge or trial.

Jack Mapanje was arrested by police at the Gymkhana Club in Zomba on 25 September 1987. Since then he has been detained in Mikuyu Prison in southern Malawi. For almost two years he was not allowed visits from friends, nor was he allowed to see his wife and three children. More recently, however his wife has reportedly been allowed to visit him at about two monthly intervals. Little is known about the conditions of his imprisonment.

Since no charges have been brought and no public statement made it is only possible to speculate about the reasons for his detention. Although Jack Mapanje is not believed to have been overtly politically active or to have been connected with any opposition group, his recent poetry has increasingly dealt with political themes. After his arrest the police searched his office at the University of Malawi and seized various manuscripts including copies of his recently banned collection of poems, "Of Chameleons and Gods". It is likely that the authorities were also concerned about his plans to bring out a second volume of poems, provisionally entitled "Out of Bounds".

The Malawian Government has not responded to Amnesty International's enquiries about the precise reason for his arrest and the legal basis for his detention, but it appears that Jack Mapanje is being held under a detention order signed by Life-President Dr H Kamuzu Banda. Under the 1965 Public Security Regulations the President can order the indefinite detention without charge or trial of anyone "for the preservation of public order". The President is supposed to review detention orders every six months but there is no obligation on the government to publish details of the reasons for detention or the results of the reviews, if they take place. Detainees have no opportunity whatsoever to challenge their continuing imprisonment.

Jack Mapanje is one of a large number of political prisoners in Malawi. He has been detained without charge or trial for his peacefully held opinions and apparently because of official disapproval of his work. His case has attracted widespread international attention because of his stature as a poet and theoretical linguist both inside Malawi and beyond.

Torture

In many countries, people are arrested and tortured – either by physical violence (e.g. beatings or electric shocks) or by mental cruelty (e.g. having mock executions to make them think that they are about to die, or depriving them of sleep). Although torture is against the law, many governments secretly allow it to continue.

Some people argue that torture is necessary in order to get information and therefore to protect innocent people. In fact, this seldom happens. Information obtained under torture is notoriously unreliable. A political prisoner may be tortured in order to make him or her sign a false confession, or to break his or her resistance. Amnesty argues that there can be no justification for inflicting pain on a defenceless prisoner. Torture is universally condemned, under international law, because it goes against our common humanity.

When Amnesty hears of a case of torture, it gets its members to write to the authorities, protesting about this. They ask that the prisoner, or prisoners, should receive proper medical attention, and that their safety should be guaranteed. As a result of this sort of public pressure, individual cases of torture have been stopped, and in some countries it has led to a change in the way in which all prisoners are treated when they are arrested.

Urgent action appeals

If there is an urgent need – if someone is about to be executed, or there is a fear of torture, or someone has disappeared – Amnesty goes into action quickly. Within twelve hours of the news coming to Amnesty over the telex, the Urgent Action Team sends out over a hundred messages round the country, giving details of each case and suggesting the form which the telegrams and letters of protest should take. About 6,500 individual people in Britain, and many school-based groups, help with urgent action appeals. They provide money for telegrams and telexes, and write letters. During 1989, the urgent action appeal went out 530 times, on behalf of more than 2,000 prisoners.

66 *When the first 200 letters came, the guards gave me back my clothes. Then the next 200 letters came and the prison director came to see me. The letters kept coming: 3,000 of them. The President called the prison and told them to let me go.* 99

When this happens: —

Amnesty responds like this:—

A time of change

Dan Jones thinks that one of the exciting things about the human rights movement today is that it really does have the power to influence what happens in many different parts of the world. We live in times of rapid change – even by the time you read this book, the political situation in some countries will have changed since it was written.

To meet the challenge of the future, Amnesty International works with many different groups of people. It has organisations for students, teachers, doctors and lawyers. It also has a network of young people who belong to Amnesty in school groups. There are more than 300 of these. They receive a magazine each term called *New Release*, and have their own campaigns.

The death penalty

Today, 40 per cent of countries do not use capital punishment at all. About 80 per cent of executions take place in just a few countries: Iran, Iraq, Nigeria, South Africa, China, the USA and the Soviet Union. In 1989, Amnesty received reports that 2,826 people had been sentenced to death in 62 countries. It also heard of 2,229 executions carried out in 34 countries.

Amnesty International opposes all use of the death penalty, whether it is for criminal offences or political ones. It also condemns the way in which thousands of people sometimes 'disappear' or are murdered for their political views, without ever coming to a court, or being charged with any offence. Amnesty argues that the value of all human life is lessened in any country where prisoners are treated badly or executed, even if the government claims that it executes people in order to protect its citizens from them.

Amnesty argues that it is contradictory for a country to say that murder is the worst crime that a person can commit, and then go on to use execution as the punishment for that crime – for that involves doing the same thing as the murderer, but this time doing it in the name of society as a whole.

In practice, the death penalty occurs in three situations:

1 The execution by law of those who have committed political offences, or who are dissenters (i.e. they protest about the political system).

2 The execution of political figures or ordinary citizens outside the rule of law, by state security forces or pro-government death squads.

3 The execution of criminals found guilty of violent crimes or, in some countries, of sexual crimes.

Using execution as a means of trying to silence political opposition does not automatically lead to peace. It may deepen people's resentment of their government, and this may bring about even more social conflict and bloodshed.

Amnesty also argues that the death penalty for a particular crime does not actually deter other people from committing the same sort of crime. Comparisons of the crime figures in countries that have retained or abolished the death penalty do not show that crime is lessened by the threat of a death sentence.

> **66** *It always surprises me that some people agree with the death penalty, although they are against torture. If I describe torture using electric shocks, or people being given drugs until they go mad, or having their bones broken, everyone says that it is terrible. But what if I tell you about a system where you don't just break people's arms or legs, but their necks; where you don't just give an electric shock that will hurt, but which will kill; where you give drugs which are lethal? Isn't that even worse?* **99**

> **66** *The idea of capital punishment doesn't deter a murderer.* **99**

> **66** *The death penalty is the ultimate form of cruel, degrading treatment for prisoners, whatever they have done.* **99**

In any legal system there can be mistakes. The problem of the death penalty is that it is final. If a mistake is made, it cannot be put right afterwards.

Over to you

1 Compose a letter to the president of an imaginary country, asking him to release a prisoner who is being held without trial. You know that the prisoner criticised the government in an article that she wrote for a newspaper. Explain to the president why you think he should not have arrested her in the first place, and why she should not be held without trial. (It would be better to write to a *real* president about a *real* prisoner! If you would like to do so, Amnesty can provide you with information and letter-writing guides.)

2 List the reasons why you think a third of the world's governments still torture prisoners, then write down the arguments that can be made against the use of torture.
   ● Do you think that the arguments against torture are strong enough to counter the reasons why governments use it?
   ● Is there any situation in which you think it would be right to torture someone?

3 'The death penalty has never been shown to have a special deterrent effect.' Here are three different situations in which a murder is committed:
   (a) At home, in a fit of anger, a husband and wife attack one another, and one of them is killed.
   (b) A terrorist risks his or her own life in order to plant a bomb, which kills a political opponent.
   (c) An armed robber kills a security guard during a raid.
   ● Do you think that any of these people would have been deterred from committing their crime if they could have faced the death sentence?
   ● Would the idea of a life sentence in prison be less of a deterrent than death?

4 Do you know what your rights are? Look up the Universal Declaration of Human Rights adopted by the United Nations, and other international agreements. Also try to find out what your political and legal rights are in this country. Make a list of these rights. Try to find a case where someone claims that his or her rights have been abused (in the newspaper, perhaps), and then note down which of your list of rights that person has been denied.

Address for further information:

Amnesty International
British Section
99–119 Rosebery
Avenue
London   EC1R 4RE
Tel: 071–278 6000

Amnesty International can supply a whole range of educational materials about human rights. Write to the above address for further details.

Sudarshan Abrol

HELPING HANDICAPPED CHILDREN

Sudarshan Abrol is headteacher of Mayfield School in Brimingham, a special school for children who are mentally and physically handicapped, with learning difficulties. She is from a Sikh family, and brings to her work the Sikh principle of service to the community and the belief that all people are of equal value. She is a champion of the rights of women, particularly those of the Asian community, and of the handicapped. She wants her pupils to learn the skills that will enable them to become as independent as possible, but she also wants society to learn to value handicapped people, and to understand that, in spite of their physical or learning difficulties, they have a great deal to contribute. In 1988, she was awarded the MBE by the Queen for her work with the handicapped, and with women and girls in the Asian community.

Sudarshan Abrol was born and brought up in the Punjab, in North-West India. She wanted to be a teacher, but didn't belong to a rich family, so she had to work in the mornings and study in the evenings. Eventually she gained a postgraduate qualification as a teacher, and became an assistant inspector of schools.

When she arrived in England in 1963, she had the advantage of speaking English well because she had done her studies and examinations in English. This enabled her to get a teaching post, and for four years she taught infants. In 1965, she and her husband decided to visit India – they were feeling homesick and wanted their parents to see their young daughter, Gurinder, who was fifteen months old. Before going, Gurinder had to have a vaccination against smallpox. It is very rare for a person to react badly to a vaccine, but Gurinder did, and as a result her left side was paralysed. She had physiotherapy (treatment using exercises and massage), and was able to go to an ordinary school, along with children who were not handicapped. It was this that led Sudarshan Abrol to start working with children who have special educational needs.

Schools in India and Britain

Children in big cities or towns in India, or in private schools, may have quite a formal education, with traditional discipline. But for children in remote villages, the situation may be quite different. There is no compulsory education across the whole of India, and there may be no proper school building for them. They may not have classrooms, but receive lessons in the open air, under the trees. When children from villages like this arrive at a British school, they may find it very difficult to be confined to the four walls of a classroom, or to follow the routine of school life. They do not understand what is expected of them. Teachers think that they are behaving strangely, but do not know why.

Some children go into special reception centres when they first arrive from Asian countries, so that they can get used to things before being put into different schools. Mrs Abrol once had a phone call from a reception centre because they did not understand how to handle one of their pupils. When it rained, he went outside, danced around and made faces through the window, distracting the other children.

> He's celebrating the fact that it's raining!

> But it always rains in Birmingham!

> Where he comes from, rain is rare. People feel that rain is something they want to go out and celebrate.

She believes it is important to understand where people come from, and what they have been brought up to expect. A child may behave in a way that seems bizarre to people in Britain, but there may be a perfectly reasonable explanation for it.

> 66 *I remember one youngster from the Muslim side of the Punjab. He was ten, but had never been to school. He was quite intelligent, and could express himself well, but he did not understand class discipline, and tried to climb out of the window! The teachers did not understand, but I said, 'Of course he did that. He thinks you are confining him and putting him in a prison.'* 99

Mayfield School

The school has children with severe learning difficulties, and also those who are physically handicapped. Mrs Abrol does not like to put these children into separate categories because each child is unique, and has a special set of needs. Many of her children have multiple problems.

Mayfield has children as young as two years old, right through to those of nineteen. Their needs vary according to their age and the sort of problems they have. Some children come to the school while they are still in nappies, and need help with toilet training. Most of the children need help with the basic skills of day-to-day life – getting around, feeding, dressing and undressing.

She has a whole range of ability levels, from those who are able to do very little, to those who have moderate learning difficulties and are getting ready to try going to an ordinary school. This is something she encourages. In the past, it was usual for children to stay in the special school, and this is still the case with many of them. The problem

66 *We should not try to keep children here for ever, but move them on when they are better able to cope.* **99**

There is to be a Paramedic Department attached to Mayfield School. This will offer hydrotherapy (exercises in water), physiotherapy and speech therapy. At present the school has visiting staff, and children go to the local hospital for these activities. But the school has started a campaign to have all the facilities actually on the school premises. The school needs to raise a quarter of a million pounds to help with that, and it is hoped that the new Paramedic Department will be operating from 1991/2 onwards.

Pupil and helper at Mayfield: the personal touch builds confidence and friendship.

with this is that, dealing with children of limited ability all the time, the teachers' expectations of what a child can do tend to be lowered, and the more able children are not stretched to the limits of what they can do.

Every year, the progress of each child is reviewed and, if there are signs of progress, then he or she may try working for part of the time in one of the neighbouring schools. Some of the youngsters at Mayfield are profoundly handicapped, and they stay on until, at the age of nineteen, they can go to an adult training centre.

Mayfield aims to give children a practical education. They need to learn the basic skills of life in order to become independent. When Mrs Abrol talks about independence, some parents ask, 'Does that mean that he (or she) will be able to walk, or to get a job?' With some children this cannot be possible, so she prefers to speak of *inter*dependence. We all need one another's help, but she hopes that the children will become less and less dependent upon adults to do everything for them. A child who can go to the toilet and get dressed may still need to have adults around, but has already achieved some independence.

It would be ideal if you could have one teacher for each child, then you could teach each of the children individually, but Mayfield has a staffing ratio of one teacher to eight children. As well as the qualified teaching staff, there are special school assistants. Some of these are parents, others are people who have chosen to help. They all have some sort of community care qualification or experience – either looking after their own handicapped children, or caring for other relatives.

Sometimes there may be one teacher and one assistant in a classroom; at other times there could be three assistants. It all depends on the needs of the pupils. One child might be working on a one-to-one basis with a teacher, another might have a computer to operate, and another might be learning a practical skill with the help of an assistant. There will be many different activities, with teachers or assistants, going on at the same time – and each of them can contribute to the education of that particular child.

The school tries to raise extra money to pay for some of the special facilities that the children need because of their various handicaps. Parents help to raise funds, but the school is in a poor area.

The parents of handicapped children

The stress on the families of these children can be enormous. To have a handicapped child with you twenty-four hours a day is not easy. You need to have some relief, and to talk to other people about your problems and your feelings. Business people are often too busy to get this kind of support.

Some of the parents are not employed, and are desperately short of money. An attendance allowance is paid to those who have to stay at home to care for a handicapped person, and there is also child benefit – but it is not enough for some families. At least these allowances help the child to be accepted, for otherwise he or she would be a financial burden. Often, the main effort of caring for a child falls on the mother, and she gets little support.

In spite of the frustrations, there is a great deal of care given within the family, sometimes by brothers and sisters, and that is good. Some handicapped children are over-protected by those who care for them, and are not encouraged to do enough for themselves.

There is a parents' group at Mayfield School, where people can help one another, and become involved with what is being done for their children. There is also a social surgery, where parents are helped to sort out any benefits to which they are entitled.

Equal opportunities?

Sudarshan Abrol argues that Asian girls who have a physical handicap, or learning difficulties, can suffer three times over:

1 Women are at a disadvantage compared with men in our society. The majority of top jobs still go to men. The real contribution that women make in the home is not recognised. Few institutions have pre-school playgroups so that women can return to work after having children if they want to.

2 If you are a black or Asian woman, the situation is worse. Within the Asian community itself, women suffer oppression. Some work in the home, when they might

> **" Some parents find that it is very difficult to accept that they have a handicapped child. They may feel guilty; especially mothers. They may ask, 'Why have I been given this handicapped child? Why does God test me in this way?' "**

> **" We try to get the parents into the school as much as possible. "**

prefer to use their qualifications to take up a career, because their men want to remain in charge of bringing in the family income. If a woman speaks out about these things, she is unlikely to be popular. Men may reject her because she is outspoken, because she has a brain and because she won't take nonsense from them! Within society as a whole, Sudarshan Abrol feels that people often take little notice of what Asian women have to say.

3 If you are disabled as well, things are worse still. There are few opportunities for the handicapped to enjoy themselves after school, or to have a social life. There are also very few single-sex establishments for Asian girls, although that is what they prefer. When it comes to getting a job, handicapped people have to work extra hard to try to prove what they can do.

Asian women in Britain – do they enjoy equal opportunities? Sudarshan Abrol thinks not, and campaigns on their behalf.

Among the Asian community, parents are particularly concerned that their daughters should avoid sex before marriage. A girl who gets pregnant before marriage is likely to be condemned by her society. Because of this, many parents prefer that girls – especially those who are mentally handicapped – should be able to go to single-sex establishments, but Mrs Abrol points out that, at the moment, there is no provision for this in her area, and she has been unable to persuade the authorities to provide it.

66 *Asian parents are keen that the mentally handicapped girls should be cared for in single sex hostels, and looked after by women.* 99

Sex is a natural instinct that we all share – and that includes those who are handicapped. Children have to be taught what sort of behaviour is socially acceptable and what isn't, but this is difficult for those with learning

37

difficulties. Such girls are particularly vulnerable because they are mature physically, but may be unable to know what is the right thing to do.

So why is there no provision for these girls? Is it because there is no real need for it, or because, where Asian handicapped girls are concerned, society is prepared to turn a blind eye? What should the priorities be when money is allocated for schools? These are the sort of questions Sudarshan Abrol constantly asks.

Asian children and Western culture

Sudarshan Abrol believes that teachers should give children a balanced view of their own culture and the culture they are mixing in. For example, they need to be taught about the arranged marriage system which operates in Asian cultures, and compare it with the way in which young people in the West choose their marriage partners. Teachers should be able to disucss the good and bad points of both systems, and youngsters should be able to decide for themselves what is right for them.

Young people have learnt that they are free – but what is freedom? Freedom is only possible within certain social restraints. You have to know what is socially acceptable behaviour in your society, and you have to act within that.

More work has to be done to educate people. Asian and black people need to know that they have rights. They have come to this country, and have learned English, and they are then expected to keep the law – but often they do not know what their rights and duties are under the law.

The Sikh religion

One of the most important things in the Sikh religion is that all people are to be treated equally, whether they are rich or poor, and whatever social class they belong to.

The Sikh religion teaches equality of men and women, and women have a high status in the religion, but in practice it may be different. Although they are allowed to conduct worship, and to read from the Guru Granth Sahib (the Sikh holy book), in some gurdwaras (Sikh temples) women are not encouraged to do so. This is an example of social oppression working against women, and, Mrs Abrol argues, it is found in all sections of the community.

66 *They are pretty looking; they could win anybody's heart: that is why they are vulnerable.* 99

66 *Freedom is not just do whatever you like. You can't walk around naked in the street!* 99

66 *It's not the youngsters' fault – they are often confused.* 99

66 *Everywhere, I go for unity. To me all children are alike – rich or poor. That influences everything.* 99

The Sikh religion also stresses that people should offer service to humanity, and Sudarshan Abrol finds that she gets satisfaction from helping out, in many different situations. This is not confined to the school – even in the evenings, people ring her up and ask for help.

Over to you

1 Imagine that you have arrived for your first day at school in a foreign country. You do not understand a word of the language, and cannot even try to pronounce words that you see written because they are in a script different from your own. No one at the school understands you.
   ● What would you need to know in order to get through the day at school?
   ● How would you make yourself understood?

2 Do you think it is best for handicapped children to stay in special schools, or to go to an ordinary school along with children who are not handicapped? List the advantages and disadvantages of each choice. In drawing up your lists, you may want to distinguish between those who are physically handicapped and those who have learning difficulties, and also between those who are mildly handicapped and those whose problems are more severe.

3 Do you agree with Mrs Abrol that women, the handicapped and members of ethnic minority groups may all find themselves at a disadvantage in British society? Give reasons for your answer, and (if you agree) suggest practical steps that could be taken to overcome these problems.

4 Everyday things we use – from cars to knives and forks – sometimes have to be adapted for use by physically handicapped people.
   ● Try to find something which has been adapted, and describe how and why it is different.
   ● Working as a group, design a toy, a game, or some simple tool that could be used by a handicapped person. You will need to decide what sort of handicap the person you are designing it for will have (e.g. he or she may have the use of only one hand).

5 Devise your own sign language. Think of a few simple signs that could be understood easily by people around the world who have no knowledge of your own language.

Address for further information about Mayfield School and the Paramedic Department project:

Mayfield School
Finch Road
Birmingham   B19 1JH

Bob Geldof

FEEDING THE WORLD

In 1984, the pop singer Bob Geldof, overwhelmed by news reports of the famine in Ethiopia, was determined to do something to help those who were starving. Using his experience and contacts in the pop music world, he launched Band Aid with the record 'Do they know it's Christmas?' Its success led him to become involved full time, helping to see that the money raised was used to help those most in need, and organising the world's largest pop concert – Live Aid. Although Bob Geldof has returned to working as a pop musician, Band Aid continues to help those who are threatened by drought and famine in Africa.

Bob Geldof was born in Dublin in 1952. The secondary school he went to was very strict, and he hated it. It was run by Catholics, and he often found himself in trouble for challenging and questioning the religious instruction he was given. His work went downhill, and he ended up failing his leaving certificate examinations. He was glad to leave, but had no idea about what to take up as a career.

After school, he had a string of jobs. He worked in a pea-processing factory in Lincolnshire, and a coffee bar and a photo-processing plant in Dublin, and he taught English as a Foreign Language in Spain. For a while in 1971 he worked as a labourer on the construction of the M25 motorway, driving one of the huge earth-moving vehicles. He just drifted from one thing to the next, with no real plan for his life.

He had always been interested in music, and, while staying in Canada, he started writing about pop music for local papers and magazines. For the first time in his life, he had work that gave him satisfaction and self-respect, as well as earning him money.

In 1975, back in Dublin, he formed the Boomtown Rats, and started his career as a pop singer. To begin with, the

> 66 *The news report was of famine in Ethiopia. The pictures were of people who were so shrunken by starvation that they looked like beings from another planet. Their arms and legs were thin as sticks, their bodies spindly . . . The images played and replayed on my mind. What could I do?* 99

> 66 *I had no hopes when I left, no ambitions, no clue as to what I should do.* 99

group could not make a living from their music, but had to take other jobs as well. Bob Geldof did a bread round for three mornings a week. Success came quickly. By 1978 the Boomtown Rats were the best-selling pop group in Britain. In that year he met Paula Yates, who was to become his girlfriend and later his wife.

66 *The Boomtown Rats became enormously successful and were then eclipsed. If the Rats had still been a success I might never have managed to start out on the enterprise which led to that perfect day in July 1985 (the day of the Live Aid concert).* **99**

In the pop music industry it is difficult to be successful all the time. In the autumn of 1984, Bob Geldof had been on tour with the band – giving forty-four performances in forty-eight days – but was having trouble selling the records.

The famine in Ethiopia

One evening in October, returning home depressed about the release of his latest single, he and Paula watched the BBC news – it included a report by Michael Buerk on the drought and famine in Ethiopia.

Life had always been hard for the people of Ethiopia and its neighbouring countries. In 1984 the rains (which usually came in March and September) failed once again. The drought had been getting worse over the previous ten years, and the people had no reserves of food. They depended on those rains in order to grow their crops, and there was no harvest.

In October, the relief centre at Alamata in northern Ethiopia reported that it was struggling to keep 100,000 people alive, but that every day between ninety and a hundred of them (mostly children) died. At Korem, 10,000

Those who were starving made their way to relief centres in the hope of getting food. They waited out in the open, with only thin clothing and sheets to keep themselves warm at night. During the day it became unbearably hot. Some received the limited supplies of food; others just sat or lay on the ground in despair, waiting to die.

66 *The worst thing was the look in their eyes. They were glazed, blank, vacuous. They looked but did not see. They were the eyes of people who had given up.* 99

This child, at a relief centre in Korem, northern Ethiopia, is too weak to eat. He is being fed through a nasal tube, provided by the Save the Children Fund emergency programme.

people had been going hungry in March; now it was up to 100,000. At Mekelle, 90 miles further north, 80,000 people were camped around the town, waiting for food. Some of the children were being fed on a special high-energy diet of powdered milk and biscuits, but every day hundreds more were arriving, and there was not enough to go round.

The government in Ethiopia estimated that drought had affected 7.7 million people (out of a population of 33 million) and that 5.5 million of them were facing starvation.

Many organisations were trying to help. At the beginning of November 1984, Oxfam announced that its appeal for Ethiopia had reached £1 million. International aid was arriving, but for many it was too late. The situation in Ethiopia was made worse by civil war. In the northern provinces of Tigre and Eritrea, guerrilla groups were fighting to gain independence from the government in Addis Ababa. Much of the food was limited to areas controlled by the government, although Oxfam and the International Red Cross were getting supplies to the rebel areas of Tigre by sending them in by road at night from the Sudan.

At the end of November, the League of Red Cross Societies in Geneva appealed for $18 million, and the European Economic Community agreed to provide another £20 million for food and air transport. Aid was pouring into Ethiopia, but some was getting blocked at the airports because there was a shortage of trucks to move it to the famine areas. By November, 7,500 children were being fed at Korem, but for many it was too late – about forty died each day.

Band Aid

Bob Geldof was horrified by the news reports, and by the pathetic helplessness of those who were literally dying in front of the television cameras. That night he could not sleep, turning all those images of starvation over in his mind.

The television report had described it as 'a famine of biblical proportions'. Bob Geldof thought it was terrible that, 2,000 years after Christ, something like this could still happen. With all our modern technology, there must be a way of preventing it. To allow it to continue, and not to do everything possible to stop it, would be the equivalent of murder.

At first he thought that he should give some money. Then he thought of giving the profits of the next record to Oxfam – but that didn't seem to be enough, either. What else could he do?

That day he came up with the idea of doing a record for Ethiopia, and thought that it should involve more than just the Boomtown Rats. He started contacting others in the pop world, and found that they all responded positively, and were prepared to join him. It took about four weeks to contact all the people, to write and adapt the music and words (which he did with Midge Ure), and to arrange the publicity and finance.

In 1984, a total of 458,000 tonnes of grain was given to Ethiopia. In 1985, because of the drought, this was raised to 1,303,000 tonnes.

The problem was not limited to Ethiopia. The Sudan also faced a severe famine. Thousands of nomads, having sold all their cattle to buy food, were sitting along the roads with nothing at all, just waiting to die. Refugees from Ethiopia were crossing into the Sudan in the hope of finding food.

In the morning, he found that Paula had stuck a note on the fridge: 'Ethiopia. Everyone who visits this house from today onwards will be asked to give £5 until we have raised £200 for famine relief.'

The recording took place on Sunday, 25 November 1984. Those who gathered for the recording included Sting, Paul Weller, Marilyn, Paul Young, Duran Duran, Spandau Ballet, U2, Culture Club, Bananarama, Status Quo, George Michael and Heaven 17. Boy George was missing, and was said to be in New York. Bob Geldof phoned him at his hotel room (although it was only 6 a.m. over there) and told him to get on the 9 a.m. Concorde for London. He did – and arrived in time to join in the recording! 'Do they know it's Christmas?' went straight to number 1 on the charts when it was released. The record itself made a total of £8 million.

Because he had promised that all the money raised would go to Ethiopia, Bob Geldof was reluctant simply to hand cash over to the existing relief agencies, who would use some of it to maintain their organisations. He therefore agreed to go out to Addis Ababa himself to see what was needed, after newspapers had agreed to cover the cost of his hotel, and TV AM had paid for his flight. At the airport in Addis Ababa he met Mother Teresa.

66 *We were printing 320,000 copies a day and still it wasn't enough. Every record factory in Britain, Ireland and Europe was pressing it.* 99

66 *She began to tell me about her work in Ethiopia. Her nuns were working in the shanty towns of the capital and they also ran a feeding centre and hospital at Alomata.* 99

He was taken to some of the relief centres, and saw people queuing for the food – a milky, high-energy porridge. Some of them couldn't manage to eat it because any sort of food hurt their stomachs after starving for so long. He also saw market stalls full of valuables, sold by people in a last desperate attempt to get money for food.

He called together representatives of the charities that were already working there, like Oxfam and Save the Children Fund, and asked them to draw up a list of the

Bob Geldof also spoke to politicians and other people in authority – both in the countries needing aid, and in those able to give it, like Britain, America and the EEC – challenging them to do everything possible to help those who were suffering.

> 66 *I simply represented a moral point of view. I wasn't seeking anyone's vote, so no one had a hold over me, and I could say and do as I liked, provided it was responsible.* 99

things they most needed, so that these could be bought by Band Aid. He saw that lorries were needed to transport food to the stricken areas, and that he would need to charter ships in order to deliver his supplies, and those of other agencies. Of the money raised for Band Aid, 20 per cent was used for immediate relief, 20 per cent for shipping and transport, and the rest for long-term development projects to try to prevent other famines in the future.

The Live Aid concert

> 66 *All of my life I felt like I had been waiting. For what I was unsure. Things felt good or bad, but never complete. There was always something else – something unspecific. Not today. Had all the waiting been for this? Was this it?*
>
> *'I think this must be the greatest day of my life,' was all I could find to say.* 99

Live Aid – the biggest pop concert ever – took place on 13 July 1985. Fifty-two performers in Britain, the USA and the Soviet Union were linked by satellite. It started in Wembley Stadium in Britain at noon. During breaks in the performances, pop groups from other places, including the Soviet Union, were screened. Then from 5 p.m. until 10 p.m. songs in Wembley alternated with those in the JFK Stadium in Philadelphia. After 10 p.m. the American concert continued for another five hours. There were 72,000 people (including the Prince and Princess of Wales) at Wembley, and 90,000 at Philadelphia, but the concert was also beamed by fourteen international satellites to 500 million television sets around the world. The total audience was estimated to be 1.5 billion.

On the Monday morning after Live Aid, people queued up outside banks and post offices, waiting to donate their money. The total raised around the world by the Live Aid concert was over £50 million.

*The following year, Bob
Geldof was involved with
Sport Aid. On Sunday, 25
May 1986, 10 million people
took part in a sponsored run,
over a 6-mile course. It took
place in 278 cities across
seventy-eight different
countries. It was called 'The
Race Against Time' because
people realised that, with
every passing day, more and
more people were dying
because of lack of food.
Around the world, Sport Aid
raised another £50 million.*

Aid continues

The problems of drought and famine are not solved by a
single appeal for help, however successful. People soon
became aware that Africa needed long-term help to tackle
its food crisis. Many other 'Aid' appeals were launched
around the world, inspired by what had been done at Live
Aid. Band Aid itself continued to receive money and to use
it to help charities and others who were working in the
famine areas, and to fund projects for long-term
development.

In 1989 the harvests failed once again in northern
Ethiopia. The 488,000 tonnes of grain given that year were
not enough, and it was estimated that 1 million tonnes
would be needed in 1990 to prevent further starvation. For
Christmas 1989 Band Aid released its second recording of
'Do they know its Christmas?' Some of those taking part –
like Cliff Richard – had been in the pop music business for
a long time, but others – like Kylie Minogue and Jason
Donovan – were still at school when the first Band Aid
record was released!

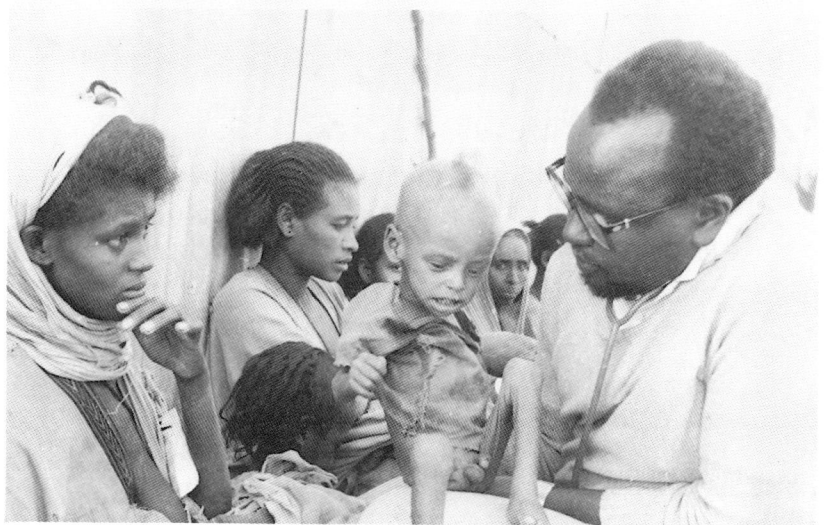

*This Kenyan doctor examines
a starving baby at a relief
centre in Ethiopia. People
continue to suffer in Africa,
even when their plight does
not make the newspaper
headlines.*

Food and Africa

Although Africa continues to grow more food, it is not
enough to keep up with the increase in its population,
which is expected to reach over one billion by the year
2010. Poor people tend to have large families, in the hope

In 1986 Bob Geldof was made an honorary Knight of the British Empire (KBE). The award citation said:

He has had a major impact on raising awareness in Britain of Africa's continuing problems. As a result of his personal efforts through the Band Aid organisation and the Live Aid concerts, some £38 million have already been raised in Britain for emergency famine relief.

The address of Band Aid is:

Band Aid Trust
P.O. Box 4TX
London   W1A 4TX

that their children will help them with their work, and also look after them in their old age. The wealthier people become, the fewer children they need.

Over half of Africa, the rainfall is not enough to support the growing of crops, and it tends to vary from year to year. In areas like northern Ethiopia, people are just about able to survive if all goes well and the rains come on time.

During famines, it is estimated that the people themselves provide 90 per cent of what is needed to keep alive, by selling everything to buy food. The outside aid is only about 5 per cent of what is needed in total. But since the famine of 1984–5, many of the people have nothing left to sell, and they either receive outside help or starve.

Much of the money raised in Britain each year for the people of Ethiopia is handled by the Disasters Emergency Committee. This is made up of the five major aid organisations in Britain: Christian Aid, the Catholic Fund for Overseas Development, Save the Children Fund, Oxfam and the Red Cross.

I can't sit and watch people die on my TV!

Over to you

1 Collect information about the causes of famine in Africa, and about the sort of aid that is being given.
   ● What are the long-term needs of the people there?
   ● Do you think it is ever going to be possible to eliminate the threat of starvation because of drought? Give your reasons.

2 Find out all you can about the way in which governments give help to one another, and about the way charities work – both in emergencies and in long-term development. Why do you think Bob Geldof found that he was free to challenge people in charge of government policies, and to say things that other aid workers were afraid to say?

3 Do you think it is right for television reporters to show pictures of people who are dying, and the grief of those who mourn? Should they intrude on their lives in this way? Imagine that you have just taken such a film. Write a letter to a friend, explaining why you did so. (Or, if you think it would be wrong to film them, write saying why you refused to do it.)

Swee Chai Ang

GIVING MEDICAL AID TO PALESTINIANS

> *The Palestinian people have a dream. And I share their dream: the dream of a world just visible through the smouldering ruins of the refugee camps and the tear gas – a world where an eleven-year-old boy need not learn to use a Kalashnikov or rocket-launcher to defend his family – a world of peace, justice and security.*

In 1982, Dr Swee Chai Ang was one of about a hundred medical people from all over the world who responded to an international appeal for doctors to help treat the wounded in Beirut, following the Israeli invasion of Lebanon.

Her experience of the suffering of the Palestinians in the camps in Beirut led her, when she returned to Britain, to appeal for funds to help them, and to set up the charity Medical Aid for Palestinians (MAP).

Since then, MAP has provided medical supplies and has organised for volunteers to go out to Beirut and elsewhere to help those who are suffering. If offers medical treatment to all who are in need, whether they are Palestinians or Lebanese. Swee Chai Ang has returned to the Lebanon many times, although she and the others who volunteer know that they risk their lives in a country which is torn apart by war.

Dr Swee Chai Ang was born and brought up in Singapore. She studied medicine there, and became involved with community medicine, and then with orthopaedic surgery (the repair and treatment of damaged bones and muscles). In 1977 she and her husband moved to Britain, where she worked as an orthopaedic surgeon and also as an occupational health specialist – looking at ways in which people's work affected their health.

In the summer of 1982, the Israeli army invaded Lebanon, seeking to destroy the bases of Palestine Liberation Organisation (PLO) fighters. Swee Chai Ang had always supported Israel, and had heard of PLO terrorists, but she had never before thought of the Palestinians as people, or as victims. In Britain, newspapers and television reported that up to 100,000 people had been made homeless, and probably about

14,000 had been killed. Many thousands were crowded into camps in Beirut. Swee Chai Ang was desperately concerned about their fate, and when she heard of an appeal for an orthopaedic surgeon to go out to Beirut, she volunteered, although she knew that she might well lose her life.

Beirut in 1982

When the state of Israel was created in 1948, many of the people who were living in Palestine at that time fled. About 750,000 of them became exiles in the neighbouring countries, and some came to live in Beirut. They were packed into small areas of crowded flats and houses, divided by narrow alleyways and streets. These were called 'camps'. After the invasion, and the constant shelling, the camps were reduced to ruins.

> **66** *Seeing the wounds of the people of Lebanon hurt me, firstly because they had been inflicted by Israel, secondly because I am a Christian, and thirdly because I am a doctor.* **99**

Beirut was divided between the Christian East and the Muslim West, by what was called the 'green line'. Not all of the Palestinians in the camps were Muslim – about one-fifth of them were Christian, and there were even some Jewish families.

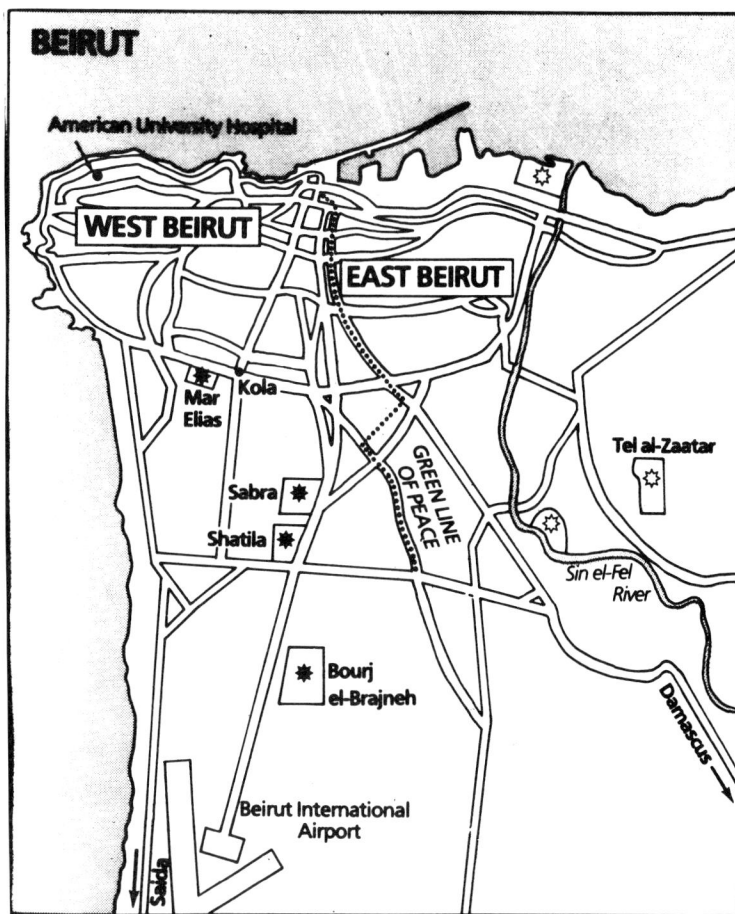

Palestinian refugee camps in East Beirut (attacked and destroyed 1974-76)

Palestinian refugee camps in West Beirut

49

There were fine hospitals in Beirut, but they were private, and anyone who did not have at least £3,000 to pay for treatment was turned away. The Palestinian Red Crescent Society (like the Red Cross) had set up hospitals offering free medical care, but nine of these had been destroyed in the Israeli invasion. Only one hospital was still standing – the Gaza – and this had no water or electricity. In nearby Akka hospital, they were trying to treat people in a ruined basement.

Soon after Swee Chai Ang arrived in Beirut, it seemed that peace would return, and the PLO agreed to move its fighting men out of Beirut. Water and electricity were restored to Gaza hospital, which served the people of Sabra and Shatila camp, and Swee Chai Ang was working there to help those who had been wounded.

The view from the Gaza hospital, looking over Sabra and Shatila camp, 1982

Then, on 15 September, the camps were sealed off from the rest of Beirut by Israeli tanks, and armed men (who did not say who they were) invaded the camps, killing their inhabitants and destroying the already ruined homes. The

Red Cross estimated that 2,400 people were killed in the camps during that raid.

Swee Chai Ang and the other medics were hauled out of the hospital, and at one stage they were lined up against a wall, and thought that they too would be shot. Then they were released and taken out of the camp. They heard that, at the nearby Akka hospital, doctors, nurses and patients alike had been shot.

She felt horrified and angry that such things could happen, and went to Jerusalem to give evidence at an inquiry into what had taken place. Then she had to return to Britain, for her contract with the charity that had sent her to Beirut had finished.

Medical Aid for Palestinians (MAP)

For some time, Swee Chai Ang went round Britain, speaking about the terrible conditions in which the Palestinian people were living. She found a great deal of support from people, and in 1984 she helped to set up a charity to send medicines and equipment to help the Palestinians. This was called Medical Aid for Palestinians. It was not to become involved in the political side of the Palestinian problem, but simply to support medical projects. It would also pay for some of the wounded to be brought to Britain for treatment.

MAP collected money from people who wanted to do something for the Palestinians, using it to pay the expenses of its volunteers and to buy medical supplies. Working from the basement of an office building in London, MAP ran mainly with voluntary helpers, and by 1987 it had sent out more than seventy medical volunteers, of ten different nationalities, to work in Lebanon. There was danger of being kidnapped, and sometimes people had to be evacuated when their lives were directly threatened. But in spite of this, more doctors, nurses and other health workers came forward to volunteer.

The rule laid down by MAP was that the volunteers should treat anyone in Lebanon who needed their help. There were enough divisions already within Lebanon, and the charity did not want to add to them.

66 *For me, supporting the Palestinians is not a political matter: it is my human responsibility. They seek to return home, Failing that, they demand the right to a decent life in exile: the right to exist.* 99

66 *Charity is not pity. The English word 'charity' originally meant 'love'.* 99

The war of the camps

> 66 *The average person in the camp might easily have twenty or thirty pieces of bomb or shell shrapnel lodged in his or her body. Small pieces were best left alone. Larger pieces of flying shrapnel from an exploding bomb or shell would often amputate a limb. With the return of relative calm, kids loved to get their shrapnel taken out so that they could compare the metal 'souvenirs' from their bodies.* 99

A young man, who had been a medical student until the invasion, showed Swee Chai Ang the destruction in Bourj el-Brajneh and asked her to explain what was happening to the Palestinians. She could find no answer to give him.

Why do people hate us Palestinians? Why do they want to destroy us like this?

For a while conditions improved, and Swee Chai Ang was pleased to hear that the Gaza hospital had been rebuilt and was operating again. But then, in May 1985, the camps were shelled, and attacked by Amal (one of the Lebanese Muslim groups). Unlike the earlier invasion, this time some of the camp people were armed, and were determined to fight back. Even young children carried guns, and knew how to use them. Soldiers closed off the Palestinian camps, and shot at those who tried to leave to get supplies.

Although her friends tried to dissuade her because it would be so dangerous, Swee Chai Ang was determined to go back to Beirut to help. So, in the summer of 1985, she and five other volunteers set out once again for the Middle East.

She found Beirut in a state of chaos, with many different groups fighting one another. It was impossible for her to return to her old camp area of Sabra and Shatila, so she went to the only working hospital – the Haifa hospital in Bourj el-Brajneh camp. The camp itself was an area of only 4 square kilometers, with damaged buildings divided by very narrow alleys, down which it was difficult for two pedestrians to pass one another without moving sideways. Yet there were 25,000 people crowded into the camp. Amal soldiers guarded all the entrances, and the people could not leave it to go for food, or even to bury their dead. The conditions for the people there were terrible.

The medical problems she encountered were horrific. Many of her patients were young men and women who had suffered gunshot wounds while defending the camps. One hundred and seventy-six people had had limbs amputated, but there was nowhere for them to go to get artificial limbs fitted. In the middle of chaos, the doctors and nurses set about organising operating theatres, getting instruments and medicines wherever they could.

In Shatila camp there was no proper hospital. The Gaza hospital, where she had worked in 1982, was ruined. She had to perform operations in people's homes, using only the simplest of medical equipment. One day, she removed a bullet from a young man's hand, with no surgical gloves or mask, and with no anaesthetic at all.

> This is going to hurt – we have run out of anaesthetics.

> Doctor, you have forgotten I am a Palestinian.

> What could I say to a patient like that?

> ❝ Lebanon has made me very sad. This place has seen too many tanks, too many guns, too many wars. Young people, instead of going to school or work, had to carry arms and fight for a living. Instead of money being spent on health and welfare, cash was being diverted into the pockets of arms dealers. ❞

She soon found that she had used up all the money that had been raised in Britain – most of it had bought an X-ray machine, and equipment for the operating theatre. She was also able to help get an ambulance on the road for patients at the Haifa hospital.

The sad thing she noticed was that people had not asked if someone was Lebanese or Palestinian in 1982 – they just worked together. But in 1985, Lebanese and Palestinian, Muslim and Christian, even Shiite Muslim and Sunni Muslim, all were divided up into separate groups, and were reluctant to help or trust one another.

Keeping hope alive

One day she arrived in Shatila camp to find the clinic closed, and all the surrounding buildings empty. Then a girl told her that the people had gone to the Shatila mosque, where they were holding a ceremony in memory of the fifty Palestinian martyrs who had died defending the camp.

> ❝ I stood there stunned: before me was a large crowd of Palestinians – men, women, children; young and old. Countless Palestinian flags were waving. Large pictures of martyrs were carried on poles and waved about. Drums were beating. Palestinian music sounded out. People were dancing and chanting militant slogans. I felt tears streaming down my face. I was crying because there was nothing but ruin and rubble all around, and so many had died, but yet today's memorial was not a

memorial of sorrow, but one of hope and triumph. How could these Palestinians celebrate so triumphantly, I asked myself. Then I realised that only a vision of victory could remove the pain of death, destruction and separation. Today there was this spirit of victory – in the midst of the broken walls and the rubble of Shatila camp, in the battered old mosque. This glorious sight – of victory, of jubilation, of confidence despite insurmountable difficulties – was something I will always cherish, and want to share with the suffering people all over the world. 99

From *Beirut to Jerusalem* by Swee Chai Ang

For forty days, shells and rockets had been fired at the crowded camp, but the people had not surrendered. Now they wanted to celebrate those who had given their lives defending it.

The siege of Bourj el-Brajneh

66 *Throughout the last six months of the siege, the market continued to see all kinds of delicious fruits, meat and vegetables, while the Palestinians in Shatila camp starved. When they asked for food, they only received bullets and mortar bombs.* 99

In January 1987, MAP received a telex from their volunteers in Bourj el-Brajneh. It said that the camp had been completely cut off for twelve weeks, and its residents were suffering terribly. Twenty thousand people were crowded into a camp only 200 yards square. There was no more food, and a desperate need for drinking water. Women had been shot trying to get water for their families. The three volunteers – Pauline Cutting (a British surgeon), Ben Alofs (a Dutch nurse) and Susan Wighton (a Scottish nurse) – appealed for international help to lift the siege and send in supplies. This message was soon followed by another, describing the starvation in the camp, and appealing to the United Nations to do something to stop the massacre of its inhabitants.

MAP decided to organise a team of volunteers to replace Dr Cutting and the others at Bourj el-Brajneh camp. They gathered about 4 tonnes of medical supplies, and a team of eight of them left for Lebanon. Unfortunately, when they reached Cyprus, Swee Chai Ang was told that the Lebanese authorities would not allow her to enter the country because she was already known as a supporter of the Palestinians. Five members of the team crossed into East Beirut, and tried to negotiate to get their supplies into the camp.

In desperation, Swee Chai Ang wrote directly to President Assad of Syria, asking him to get his peacekeeping force to move in and replace the Amal soldiers who were blockading the camps. On 6 April the Syrian forces moved in, and two days later Swee Chai Ang was on a ferry for Beirut. The Syrians allowed women to leave the camps to get food and water.

Sometimes Dr Swee Chai Ang made arrangements for Palestinians who had been injured to be sent to Europe for treatment. For example, two boys – Bilal Chebib (a Palestinian) and Samir Ibrahim el-Madany (a Lebanese) – had been hit by snipers in December 1986, and were paralysed. In July 1987 they were brought to Britain, where arrangements had been made for them to receive treatment in the Spinal Injuries Centre at Stoke Mandeville Hospital.

The boys are greeted by Dr Ang and Dr Cutting on their arrival in Britain for treatment.

(For more information about this centre, see the chapter on the work of Jimmy Savile in Book 1 of Leading the Way.*)*

She found that there were plenty of Palestinian doctors in the camps, but they needed medical supplies. Swee Chai Ang, being a foreigner, was the best person to leave the camps and cross all the military checkpoints in order to get them. She managed to get her 4 tonnes of medical supplies into the camps a bit at a time, using an old battered ambulance.

66 *The first time I drove it out of Bourj el-Brajneh camp, the Syrian soldiers at the checkpoint were astonished to see this 'thing' come out of the camp and they ran towards it. Only then did they realise that it had a driver. I was so small that they could not see me, and thought the old heap of rust had taken off on its own!* 99

66 *The physical survival of Shatila is not the point. Shatila lives in the hearts of every one of us.* 99

Shatila camp in 1987. The Palestinians continued to live among these ruins.

Shatila camp had been under siege for nearly two years, from May 1985 to April 1987.

The final destruction

The Palestinians continued to live in the Beirut camps, although they still had no water or electricity. They did not even have building material to repair the shell holes in their homes. In January 1988, things seemed to improve. Nabih Berri, leader of the Amal militia, lifted the siege of the camps. He did this as a gesture of support for the Palestinians because of the way in which the Palestinians in the Occupied Territories (the areas of the West Bank and Gaza controlled by Israel) were resisting the Israeli soldiers.

Then, in May 1988, the Palestinian camps were shelled from the mountains outside Beirut by anti-PLO forces. Both camps were flattened. Shatila finally fell on 27 June 1988, and Bourj el-Brajneh a few days later.

In 1987 Dr Swee Chai Ang met Yasser Arafat, the head of the Palestine Liberation Organisation, and he awarded her the Order of the Star of Palestine, the highest award given by the PLO, in recognition of her work.

66 *What can I say? Each time I think of Shatila, I still cry. My understanding of the Palestinians began with them. It was they who taught a naive woman surgeon the meaning of justice. It was they who inspired me to struggle incessantly for a better world. Every time I felt like giving up, they would strengthen me with their example.* 99

Address for further information:

Medical Aid for Palestinians
29 Enford Street
London   W1

The full story of Dr Ang and the Palestinians is told in her book *From Beirut to Jerusalem* (Graffon Books, 1989).

Over to you

1 Collect newspaper cuttings about the situation of Palestinians in Lebanon and elsewhere in the Middle East. Have there been any changes since the events described in this chapter?

2 MAP gives aid for humanitarian reasons. It is not a political organisation.
   ● Write down examples of what you think of as 'political' actions. Then do the same for 'humanitarian' actions.
   ● Do you think, in a situation like that in Lebanon, it is possible to be humanitarian without also being political?
   ● Can you think of other parts of the world where humanitarian aid is given in a difficult political situation?

3 Imagine that you are a young Palestinian. You know how to use a Kalashnikof rifle. A friend tells you that he or she thinks it is always wrong to kill people. Another says that you ought to defend yourself. How would you reply to each of them? Would you use your rifle – and, if so, in what circumstances?

Sangharakshita

FOUNDING A NEW BUDDHIST MOVEMENT IN THE WEST

Having read about Buddhism at the age of sixteen, Dennis Lingwood (who has the Buddhist name Sangharakshita) realised that he was a Buddhist. He travelled widely in India, and elsewhere in the East, learning from senior teachers of different Buddhist traditions, and became ordained as a monk.

In 1968, having returned to Britain, he founded the Western Buddhist Order – ordaining men and women who wanted to commit themselves to the Buddha, his teachings, and the spiritual community of fellow Buddhists. He also established the Friends of the Western Buddhist Order (FWBO), an organisation for all those who are Buddhist, or who are interested in learning about Buddhism. The FWBO now operates Buddhist centres worldwide, and promotes an approach to Buddhism which is specially suitable for those who live in the West.

> 66 *Once I realised that I was a Buddhist, it seemed that I had always been one; that it was the most natural thing in the world to be one, and that I had never been anything else.* 99

Dennis Lingwood was born in South London in 1925. When he was eight years old, doctors said that he had a serious heart condition, and that he should stay in bed. For years he could not go to school, and he educated himself by reading everything he could find – starting with the *Children's Encyclopaedia*, which he read right through several times! Eventually his heart condition vanished, but his interest in books and ideas continued, and he read widely.

At the age of sixteen he read two important Buddhist scriptures – the Diamond Sutra and the Sutra of Hui Neng – and realised that what the Buddha taught was not new to him. It was what he had known and believed for a long time, and reading it was like remembering something that he had forgotten.

I soon realised that I was opposed not only to meat eating, but to violence in any form, and that I ought never to have allowed myself to become a soldier.

> " I soon realised that I was opposed not only to meat eating, but to violence in any form, and that I ought never to have allowed myself to become a soldier. "

> " Suitcases and watches were sold. Trousers, jackets and shoes given away. Identification papers destroyed. Apart from the robes which we were to wear we kept only a blanket each and our books and notebooks. "

Sangha *is the Pali word for the Buddhist spiritual community – and is sometimes used more narrowly for those who are monks. Although he did not know it at the time, Dennis Lingwood was to live up to his new Buddhist name, by founding a new branch of the Sangha in the West.*

Two years passed before he made contact with other Buddhists, and then he started going to meetings of the Buddhist Society in London. At one of their festivals, he first repeated the 'refuges and precepts' (statements of commitment to the Buddha, his teaching, the community of his followers, and the Buddhist way of life) before a monk from Burma. This was during the Second World War, and the monk – when not dressed in an orange robe for ceremonies – was a stretcher bearer, wearing ordinary clothes and practising what he preached by caring for people in a practical way.

In 1943 Dennis Lingwood was conscripted into the army, and was trained as a wireless operator. At first he thought that the army would hinder his growing interest in Buddhism, but soon after joining, his unit was sent out to India – the land where the Buddha himself had lived and taught. While posted to India, Sri Lanka and Singapore, he was able to meet Buddhist teachers. He became a vegetarian, took up the practice of meditation, and started writing and giving talks on Buddhism.

When the war ended, he chose to stay in India, rather than return to Britain, so that he could learn more about Buddhism and live as a Buddhist. Then he took a dramatic step. In 1947 Dennis Lingwood started on a completely new way of life. Accompanied by a Bengali friend, he dyed his clothes the traditional ochre colour (saffron), gave away all his possessions, and said goodbye to his friends. Then they set out on foot to make a spiritual journey. In doing this, they were following the example of the Buddha himself, who had left his life of luxury to become a wandering holy man, seeking spiritual truth.

For several years, he literally wandered from one place to another, learning about Buddhism from different teachers. In 1949 he was given lower ordination, and a year later higher ordination, so that he was a full *bhikkhu* (a Buddhist monk). Buddhist monks take on a new name when they are ordained, and Dennis Lingwood became Sangharakshita, which means 'protector of the Order'.

After his ordination, Sangharakshita moved to Kalimpong, a town in the very north of India, on the border with Sikkim and not far from Tibet. His teacher had asked him to stay there and work for the good of Buddhism. For the next fourteen years he did this – studying, writing and teaching.

Although he had been ordained in the Theravada

Those who want to follow the Buddhist path seriously are committed to three things.

1 The Buddha

Buddhists believe that the Buddha represents the highest spiritual achievement possible for human beings. We each have a Buddha nature within ourselves, and we are free either to ignore it, or to develop and become aware of it.

2 The Dharma

This is the teaching of the Buddha. It offers guidelines about how people should live, and the spiritual disciplines that they should follow in order to become more fully awake to the truth about themselves and their world.

3 The Sangha

It is very difficult to make much progress all on one's own. The Sangha is the name given to the spiritual community in Buddhism. By sharing friendship with others who are on the same spiritual path, Buddhists find inspiration and encouragement.

tradition (which developed in Sri Lanka, Thailand and other countries in South-East Asia), he came to feel that this form of Buddhism was too concerned with the rules and regulations that monks and nuns were supposed to follow. He believed that the spiritual life depended on a person's 'going for refuge' to the Buddha (as the spiritual ideal for people to follow), the Dharma (the Buddha's teaching) and the Sangha (the community of his followers) – and you didn't have to become a monk in order to do that. He saw that it was possible to be a good monk and a bad Buddhist, and vice versa! He also found that some of the most spiritually developed lamas (religious teachers) from Tibet were married.

For many years he had worked with those who were 'untouchables' in India – people who were at the very bottom of the Hindu caste system. He saw that they gained new self-respect when they became Buddhist. This was not because they had become monks, but because they had committed themselves to a new spiritual journey, following the Buddha. He therefore saw clearly that Buddhism should not be reserved for those who wanted to be monks or nuns, but was a way of spiritual development for everyone.

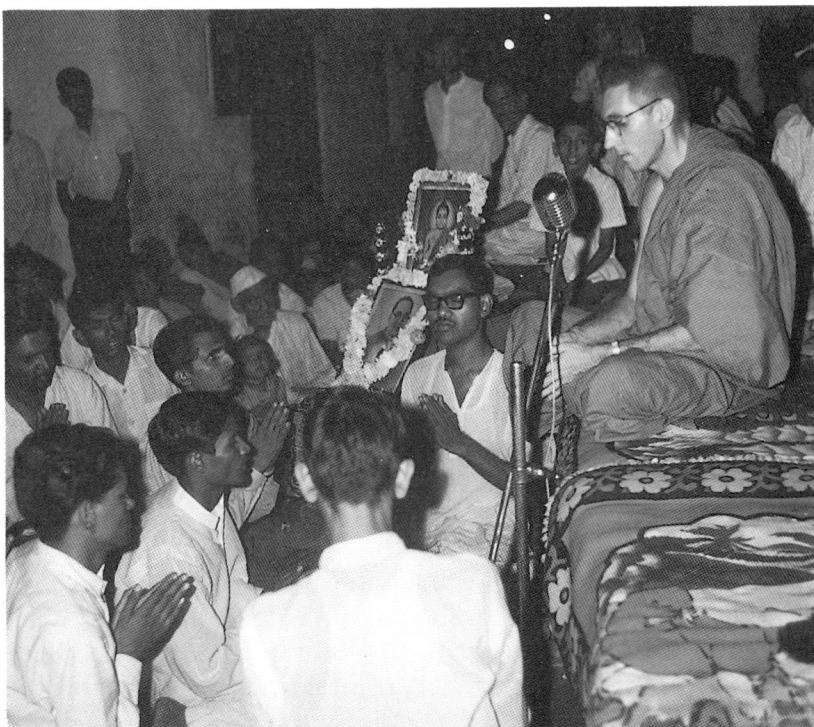

Sangharakshita with ex-untouchable Buddhists at an open air meeting in Ahmedabad, India.

60

Sangharakshita left India in 1964 and returned to Britain, in response to an invitation from the English Sangha Trust. He took up residence at the Hampstead Buddhist Vihara, and started to give lectures on Buddhism. Originally, he intended to stay only for a few months, but after two years he felt that the most important thing for him to do was to continue teaching Buddhism in the West. He therefore decided to stay in Britain, after paying a farewell visit to India.

The Friends of the Western Buddhist Order (FWBO)

From his experiences in India, Sangharakshita saw that it was important to present the teachings and practices of Buddhism in a way which would be specially relevant for people living in Western society. Buddhism in the West should not be a copy of earlier forms, but should develop in a way which would help all those who wanted to follow it. He saw that it would need to take into account the fact that people had different lifestyles – some would be married with family commitments, others would be young and single, and some would be ready to make a greater commitment to the Buddhist life than others.

On Sunday, 7 April 1968, the Western Buddhist Order was founded in a ceremony held in London, in which nine men and three women made their commitment in front of Sangharakshita to follow the path of the Buddha. Together they formed a new spiritual community. Sangharakshita also founded the Friends of the Western Buddhist Order. This is an organisation for all those who want to practise Buddhism, or who want to know more about the Buddha's teachings, and it is centred round the Western Buddhist Order. If offers spiritual friendship, training and support to everyone, whether or not they hope eventually to become members of the Western Buddhist Order itself.

The FWBO runs Buddhist centres. These offer classes in meditation, to help people to develop calmness, peace of mind and concentration. They may also have classes in physical activities, like yoga, t'ai chi or karate, and offer training in massage, to help physical relaxation and healing. Some people go to these classes without wanting

This symbol shows three flaming jewels. They stand for the Buddha, the Dharma and the Sangha.

The word Buddha *means 'one who is enlightened' or 'one who is awake'. It is the title first given to Siddhartha Gautama, who lived in the sixth century BCE. To be a Buddha is to be awake to life – to see things as they really are (including yourself); to get rid of any illusions or fantasies about life, to look at it with a clear mind, and to be able to love it with an open heart.*

66 *One cannot be what one should be merely by closing one's eyes to what one is.* 99

Tuesdays	Yoga (Beginners)	12.30 — 1.30pm
Wednesdays	Introductory Meditation Class	1.10 — 1.40pm
	Yoga (Beginners)	5.45 — 7.15pm
	Introductory Meditation Class	7.30 — 9.30pm
Thursdays	Yoga (Beginners)	5.45 — 7.15pm
	Friends' Night	7.30 — 9.30pm
Fridays	Meditation and Puja	7.30 — 9.30pm
Sundays	Meditation and Puja	8.00 — 11.00am

January

Fri 19 — Sun 21	Women Friends weekend at Rivendell	*
Fri 26 — Sun 28	Introductory weekend at Rivendell	*
Sun 28	Day event: Buddhism and Death	11am — 5pm
Tues 30	Public Talk: The Need for Myth	7.30pm

February

Fri 2 — Sun 4	Aikido weekend at Rivendell	*
Sun 4	Yoga Day	11am — 5pm
Tues 6	Public Talk: Where to Begin?	7.30pm
Fri 9 — Sun 11	Meditation Workshop at Rivendell	*
Tues 13	Public Talk: What is Religion?	7.30pm
Fri 16 — Sun 18	Introductory weekend at Rivendell	*
Sun 18	Festival: Parinirvana Day	11.00am
Tues 20	Public Talk: Buddhism as a Social Force	7.30pm
Fri 23 — Sun 25	Yoga weekend at Rivendell	*
Sat 24	Voice Workshop	2.30pm — 4.30pm
Sun 25	Musical Improvisation Workshop	11am — 5.30pm

March

Tues 6	Six week Buddhism Course begins	7.30pm
Sun 18	Introductory Day Retreat	11am — 6pm
Fri 23 — Sun 25	Yoga weekend at Rivendell	*
	Cabinet-making weekend at Rivendell	*
Sun 25	Meditation Day	11am — 6pm
Fri 30 — Sun 1	Shiatsu weekend at Rivendell	*

April

Sun 1	Painting and Meditation Day	11am — 5pm
Sat 7	FWBO Day	
Fri 13 — Mon 22	Easter Beginners Retreat at Rivendell	*
Fri 27 — Sun 29	Meditation workshop at Rivendell	*

July

| Sat 21 — Sun 29 | Beginners Retreat at Rivendell | * |

August

Sat 11 — Sun 19	Yoga week at Rivendell	*
Sat 25 — Sun 2	Beginners Retreat at Rivendell	*
	* see programme for details	

A typical programme of events at a Buddhist Centre.

An ordination ceremony.

Buddhism is a way of life and a spiritual discipline that is open to everyone. You can take from it as much or as little as you want. There is no pressure to do more than you are able – but a person who finds that his or her life is improved by Buddhist practices will want to do more, and make spiritual progress.

to understand more about the Buddhist religion itself, and they are welcome to do this. They may find that meditation helps them to cope with the stresses of modern life.

For those who want to understand more, Buddhist centres offer lectures on Buddhism, discussion groups, and opportunities to go on retreat – a time away together with other Buddhists, relaxing in the countryside, meditating and having talks and discussion.

Anyone who attends classes at a Buddhist centre is called a 'friend'. Friends can join in as much or as little as they like. Some call themselves 'Buddhist', and are committed to following the teachings of the Buddha (even if they have not yet made a public commitment to do so); others just say that they are 'interested in Buddhism'.

A person who wants to make a public commitment can apply to become a *'mitra'*. This is a Sanskrit word meaning 'friend'. Mitras try to meditate each day, to attend a class at a Buddhist centre each week, and to go on a retreat (a time of spiritual refreshment with other Buddhists) once every year. Because of their commitment, mitras share a special kind of friendship with one another, and encourage one another.

Some go on from being a mitra to ask for ordination as a 'member' of the Western Buddhist Order. This deepens the commitment taken by a mitra – Order members are expected to contribute to the work of the FWBO as much as they are able. They meet one another regularly, and try to grow spiritually, using meditation techniques. Members do not wear special robes, but when they are taking part in meditation, worship or teaching, they wear a short stole round their necks, called a *kesa*.

Some people who belong to the FWBO live together in communities. Others live on their own, or with families. There is no rule about how a person should organise his or her life – only that he or she should try to follow the teaching and example of the Buddha, and live in a way that reflects the Buddhist values of love and non-violence.

The FWBO runs a number of 'right livelihood' businesses – wholefood shops, vegetarian restaurants, health centres, bookshops and printing presses. These all reflect Buddhist values, both in what they produce and in the way those who work in them treat one another. They earn money to support the work of the centres, and also give away profits to charity. Those who work in them are paid enough to live on, but do not earn as much as they could in an ordinary business. They choose to work for the FWBO because they like working with other Buddhists, and because they feel that they are doing something worthwhile.

A member of the Western Buddhist Order, wearing a Kesa.

The Cherry Orchard Restaurant: a woman's 'right livelihood' business in Bethnel Green, London.

The Buddhist way of life

> **If you are not happy with yourself, if you are not at ease with yourself, if you don't like yourself – and many people nowadays, unfortunately, don't like themselves – you can't like other people.**

> **To be able to do one thing at a time is the whole art of life.**

> **The tragedy is not that we don't get what we want, but that we do get what we want, and then we're stuck with it, and very often we find that it's not what we wanted at all.**

A most important feature of the Buddhist life is *metta*. This means 'compassion' or 'love'. A Buddhist tries to show compassion towards all creatures – by not killing them (most Western Buddhists are vegetarian) and not stealing from them. He or she tries not to exploit other people, whether sexually or by getting money from them, to speak the truth to them, and to wish them well. One of the meditation practices offered to those who go to FWBO centres is called *Metta Bhavana* – a way of increasing a person's feeling of friendliness and compassion towards other people and all living beings. And, of course, you cannot love others unless you are also able to love yourself. Building self-awareness and self-confidence is therefore and important part of Buddhist practice.

A person who wants to understand the truth about life, and eventually to achieve enlightenment, cannot do so if his or her mind is clouded by alcohol or drugs. Buddhists therefore try to avoid these. They practise 'mindfulness', training the mind to concentrate on one thing at a time – rather than rushing from one thought to the next, in a kind of confused panic. Learning how to be still and calm is an important first step to making personal spiritual progress.

Buddhism offers a spiritual goal to which people can aspire, and it offers them practical steps that they can take in order to work towards achieving it. By doing this, it gives them a 'refuge' to which they can go. Buddhists believe that everyone goes to a refuge of some sort, in order to make sense of his or her life. Some take refuge in their careers, some in their husbands or wives, some in money or success. They think that, when they once achieve what they want, they will then be content for the rest of their lives. Sadly, their refuges generally tend to be false ones – even if they do achieve what they set out to do, it may not make them completely happy. The Buddhist believes that a person finds satisfaction when he or she goes for refuge to the Buddha, the Dharma and the Sangha, rather than to dreams of money or fame.

We each have responsibility for how we choose to spend our lives, and we have to live with the consequences of our choices, whatever they are.

How do you recognise a Western Buddhist?

Many people in Britain, when they think about Buddhism, still assume that it is about Oriental people wearing robes. There is some truth in this, for there are communities of people from other parts of the world – from Thailand, Sri Lanka or Tibet, for example – who live in Britain, but continue the Buddhist traditions of their countries of origin. Their monks still wear the traditional robes because that is what they prefer, and it is important for them to remember the culture and religion of their homeland.

Unless you get to know them personally, or see them entering or leaving a Buddhist centre, you may never know that people are Buddhists. Members of the Western Buddhist Order may be seen in jeans and sweaters, rather than in orange robes; they may be married or single; they may work as accountants, doctors, teachers, computer analysts, chefs. A person may choose to carry on with his or her same career, or may decide to work within a 'right livelihood' project, or may change career to one which is closer to Buddhist ideas and values – a soldier or burglar might feel that a career change would help!

Today, thanks to the work of Sangharakshita and others, there is a new form of Buddhism which is specially suited to those who have been born and brought up in modern Western society.

Over to you

1 In 1947 Dennis Lingwood left everything and literally walked away from his previous life. Many religious leaders – from the Buddha to St Francis of Assisi – have done this, searching for some higher personal and spiritual goal.
   ● What thoughts might go through the mind of someone about to take this step?
   ● Write out (or act) a dialogue between two friends – one of whom wants to give everything up and start a new life, and the other of whom opposes the idea.
   ● Those who join the FWBO do not have to start by taking this sort of dramatic step. Do you think this makes it easier or harder for them to make progress in their new religion?

2 The FWBO runs 'right livelihood' businesses, based on Buddhist values. Find out more about Buddhist moral values, and then draw up two lists – one of businesses which would be suitable for Buddhists, and the other of those which would not. Make a note by each business, saying why you have put it in that list.

3 Do you agree with Sangharakshita that you can only really love other people when you are also able to love yourself? Give your reasons, and also some practical examples to illustrate this.

Address for further information:

The Office of the Western Buddhist Order
Padmaloka
Lessingham House
Surlingham
Norwich   NR14 7AL
Tel.: 050-88 310

Bruce Kent

CAMPAIGNING FOR PEACE

Bruce Kent is Chairman of the Campaign for Nuclear Disarmament, and President of the International Peace Bureau. He argues that nuclear weapons are immoral, both because it is wrong to threaten to use them, knowing the terrible destruction that they would cause, and also because he believes that the large sums of money spent on weapons could be better used in helping those who are in need. He also points out that barriers created by different political systems, are unreal. People have far more in common with one another than they realise; divisions and the threat of war are a kind of madness from which the human race needs to recover, in order to build a better and safer future for everyone.

Bruce Kent was brought up as a Roman Catholic, and went to a Catholic boarding school. Although many of his teachers were priests, he didn't know what he wanted to do with his life, and he certainly did not imagine that he would become a priest himself.

He left school in 1947, soon after the Second World War. At that time, all young men had to serve in one of the armed forces – it was called National Service. Bruce Kent therefore joined the army, and became a tank commander. He was not at all unhappy about this, and would have been prepared to fight in a war. He had no idea that he would later become a peace campaigner.

During National Service, he went back to his old school for an Easter retreat (a time of quiet, for prayer and thinking about life and religion). He was impressed by the preaching of a priest who was a Jesuit, a member of the Society of Jesus, a Catholic order. He felt that God wanted him to be ordained as a priest. This was not a decision to be

We need food, not weapons!

He's a foreigner!

She's an enemy!

But we are all part of one family!

taken in a hurry, and he agreed to go to Oxford University to study Law for three years, so that he could see if he still wanted to be ordained at the end of that time.

He then had to spend another six years at a Roman Catholic seminary (a college for the training of priests), before being ordained and starting his work as a priest in a parish in Kensington, London. While he was there, he used to see people marching to the atomic weapons research centre at Aldermaston, protesting about nuclear weapons.

At that time, he thought that a priest should be concerned only with people's religious needs, and did not see it as part of his work to be involved in any sort of political action.

In August 1969, while he was working as a university chaplain in London, he flew out to Biafra, an area of Nigeria in West Africa. It was a time of civil war in Nigeria, and the people of Biafra were starving. His plane was carrying relief supplies provided by the churches, and he had been invited to spend almost three weeks in Biafra to see what was being done to help the people there. He had been raising money for them, and was concerned about all the weapons which were being supplied to both sides in the war.

He was horrified to see people starving and begging for food. He realised that, when there is a war, the innocent – especially children and old people – are the first to suffer.

He became convinced that fighting was the wrong way to resolve differences between people, and that Christians should be internationalist – that is, they should be concerned with people of all nations, not just their own. They should try to see all people as part of God's family.

His experience in Biafra also convinced him that Christians should challenge the way in which governments organise the world in which we all live. His religious ideas led him to think about political choices that people make.

Bruce Kent believes in the importance of sharing, of forgiveness between people, of service to others, and of non-violence. He thinks it is important to understand the causes of suffering and to try to change them. It is not enough just to help individual people when they suffer.

In 1987, after being a priest for twenty-nine years, Bruce Kent left the priesthood. He felt that he should speak out about the political choices that faced Britain (there was a General Election that year), but many senior people in the

Catholic Church thought that it was wrong for a Roman Catholic priest to campaign on political issues in this way.

He thinks that many churches are nationalistic – that is, they support the political view of their country – and in times of war, Christian people on each side pray for their own forces to win. He also points out that the Churches are directly involved with military people. Each year the British government spends about £10 million on providing 300 or so chaplains (priests and ministers) for the armed forces.

Walking across Europe

East German border guards erect barriers along the Berlin Wall in 1963.

After the Second World War, Europe was divided into two parts – East and West – by a border which became known as the 'Iron Curtain'. This division ran through Germany, dividing it into East Germany and West Germany. The city of Berlin, in the eastern part of Germany, was divided into West Berlin (which belonged to West Germany) and East Berlin. Later a wall was built between these two parts of the city. It became a painful reminder of how people can become cut off from one another.

In August 1988 Bruce Kent walked 1,000 miles from Warsaw to the NATO headquarters in Brussels. Warsaw, the capital of Poland, gives its name to the Warsaw Pact. This is a group of countries, including the Soviet Union, which have an agreement to defend one another in time of war. NATO (the North Atlantic Treaty Organisation) is a similar organisation, for Western countries. Both the United States of America and Britain are members of NATO.

He handed in a letter to NATO in Brussels, the same one that he had handed in at Warsaw, asking that these military blocks should be dissolved. The next day, on his return to London, he released some paper doves in Westminster. Carried by balloons, they were to express the idea of peace.

The walk took forty-five days, and raised £70,000 for charitable projects in Nicaragua and Mozambique. Bruce Kent wanted to emphasise that the money spent on weapons could be better used in helping people.

In 1989, huge demonstrations by people campaigning for greater political freedom, and a flood of young people wanting to leave East Germany to find work in the West, forced changes in the governments of Eastern Europe. Part of the 'Iron Curtain' fortifications were taken down, and the Berlin Wall was opened, allowing people once more to move from one part of the city to the other.

Young people celebrate by climbing over the wall, watched by East German police, November 1989.

Bruce Kent points out that the cost of weapons, including nuclear weapons, means that there is less money available to help those most in need. Throughout the world, by 1988, a thousand billion dollars a year was being spent on arms.

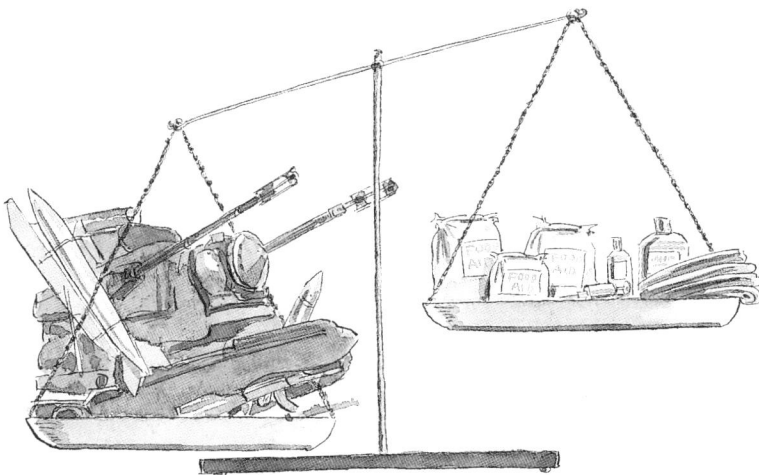

Nuclear weapons

Bruce Kent is concerned about the money that is spent on all kinds of weapons, but in particular he wants Britain to be rid of nuclear weapons. What makes nuclear weapons so special?

There are three important differences between nuclear weapons and other bombs, missiles and guns (usually called ‘conventional’ weapons):

1 Nuclear weapons are far more powerful than conventional ones. Although there are small nuclear weapons, designed to be used against tanks and other enemy forces on a field of battle, there is a danger that once these were used, both sides in the war would retaliate by using larger weapons, until the destruction would be unstoppable.

2 After the damage caused by the explosion, nuclear weapons continue to do harm to life for many years. This is because they give off radiation which can damage the cells in all living things, causing sickness and death. People are still becoming ill in Japan today as a result of the first atomic bomb, more than forty-five years ago.

There are enough nuclear weapons in the world to kill everyone many times over. By 1983 there were over 50,000 nuclear warheads – equal to almost 4 tonnes of explosives for every person. One reason why their numbers grew was called the 'arms race': both the United States of America and the Soviet Union were determined to keep pace with each other, so that neither should feel threatened.

In recent years, there have been agreements that both sides should reduce the number of their weapons. Although most people welcome these reductions, there are still far more of the weapons than could ever be used without destroying the Earth. Some people believe that the world will only be safe when all nuclear weapons are destroyed.

3 Nuclear weapons can destroy all life – plants and animals, as well as human beings – over a wide area, and their radiation can prevent new things from growing to replace those that have been destroyed. It is very difficult to control the damage that can be done by nuclear weapons, and it is possible that, if there were ever to be a nuclear war, life would be made impossible over large parts of the Earth. Some scientists suggest that, after a nuclear war, thick clouds of dust would circle the Earth, causing a dark winter that would last for years and prevent those people who survived from growing food.

A Tomahawk ship-launched cruise missile is tested off the coast of Southern California, 1985.

What should be done about nuclear weapons?

Some people believe that war can be prevented by deterrence. This means that you try to stop other people attacking you by having sufficient weapons to guarantee that anyone who tried to attack you would suffer for it. Since 1949, both the Soviet Union and the USA have developed more and more powerful or accurate nuclear weapons, in order to deter war between them.

Other people believe that nothing is achieved by having nuclear weapons. They cannot be used without endangering life on this planet, and there is always a risk that some more limited form of war will suddenly get out of hand and lead to the use of nuclear weapons, or that they will be set off as a result of an accident or misunderstanding.

The Campaign for Nuclear Disarmament (CND)

❝ *Even if there is a certain amount of rough and tumble in the school playground, you don't go around equipped with knives to carve each other up. And you know that you can't protect yourself against a boy with a knife by allowing everyone to have knives. That's the problem! You need to find a better way to sort out your disputes.* **❞**

Why go on demonstrations or wave placards? That doesn't do any good!

Demonstrating for its own sake is just silly; but sometimes it can be a useful way of getting your message across to people.

Burce Kent is the Chairman of CND. At the end of 1988 there were about 72,000 members of CND in Britain. CND believes that a country cannot be defended against attack by having nuclear weapons because they could never be used without bringing about total destruction. It argues that Britain should therefore give up its nuclear weapons.

Members of CND protest about nuclear weapons, often by going on demonstrations to draw attention to the threat they pose. They campaign for a more united world, where friendship across borders makes war less likely.

CND members want NATO to agree never to be the first to use nuclear weapons. CND would like to see all the American nuclear weapons which are kept in Britain removed.

> But there have always been wars – fighting is part of human nature!

> If you say that people will always fight because they have always fought, you might just as well say that people will always go on being cannibals because they used to be.

Bruce Kent does not believe that it is realistic to ask either the USA or the Soviet Union to give up its weapons while the other side does not. For those countries, he argues in favour of cuts in weapons, so that each may feel safe with fewer nuclear weapons to defend itself. As far as Britain is concerned, however, he believes that the country should give up its own nuclear weapons – otherwise it would only be fair for all other countries to have them as well.

Bruce Kent recognises that older people in particular find it difficult to change their ideas. Sometimes they insist that their country should be defended with the most powerful weapons possible, even if that means nuclear ones. He understands their concern, but thinks that the word 'weapon' should never have been used for a nuclear device.

73

Do religious people agree about nuclear weapons?

Almost everyone would agree with Bruce Kent that nuclear war would be a terrible thing, and that everything possible should be done to prevent it. They may disagree with him about how to achieve this.

About one-quarter of all people in CND are members of one religion or another. But there are other religious people who feel strongly that Christians should defend their freedom and the way of life that they enjoy, by fighting if necessary. They also believe that it is right to have nuclear weapons in order to deter anyone from starting a war. They share with CND members the hope that nuclear war will never happen. The difference is that they think that peace is best defended by having weapons, while Bruce Kent and other members of CND think that it is best to be rid of them.

Whatever their views on nuclear weapons, religions encourage their members to seek peace. Jesus said, "Blessed are the peacemakers, for they shall be called the children of God." Jews greet one another with the word *shalom*, which means 'peace', and Muslims say '*Salaam*', which means the same thing. Hinduism teaches non-violence, and Buddhism encourages its followers to develop a loving concern for all life, and never to kill.

Bruce Kent's hopes for the future

Bruce Kent hopes for a world in which people are able to drive through one another's countries without passports, knowing one another's languages and history, understanding one another. He wants the world to be free from the craziness of war. That involves both getting rid of weapons, and also building up trust and friendship between people of different nations.

He is now more optimistic than he used to be about the chances of world peace, and welcomes the changing attitudes of the superpowers (the Soviet Union and the USA) since Gorbachev came to power in the Soviet Union. He is encouraged by what is happening around the world. People tend not to support CND at a time when things seem hopeful, but he argues that you can't change attitudes overnight, and that there is still a long way to go before the world is made safe.

Bruce Kent is involved with politics and with the peace movement, both in this country and abroad. He is President of the International Peace Bureau. This is a network of about a hundred peace organisations from around the world, based at Geneva. It organises conferences, where people come together to discuss ways of working for peace, and it publishes information about the peace movements.

Over to you

1 What ways can you think of for promoting peace between people of different nations? Have you been abroad, on holiday perhaps?
   ● What regulations did you have to go through in order to enter those countries?
   ● What did it feel like to be a foreigner?
   ● In the past, Britain has been at war with France, Germany, Spain and Italy, but nowadays many people in Britain take holidays in those countries. What has changed?

2 Organise a debate about whether or not deterrence works. You might want to think about two things:
   ● If a person threatens to do something to you, but you think it might hurt him or her as much as you, what would you do? Would you call that person's bluff? Would you give in, rather than take the risk?
   ● Try to think of situations in which you could deter someone from attacking you, and those in which you could not. Make a list of them.

3 What are the main differences between nuclear and conventional weapons? How do these differences change the way in which these weapons could be used? Imagine you are a military commander in time of war. You have nuclear weapons, and you know your enemy has them too. In what circumstances would you seriously think about using those weapons?
   You might form your own council of war to discuss these things in a small group, and then share your conclusions with the rest of the class. If different groups come to different conclusions, try to explain carefully to one another the reasons for your decisions.)

4 have you seen any CND demonstrations, on television perhaps? What did you think they achieved? Would you want to go on a demonstration yourself? What other methods might be used to let other people know your views?

5 Do you think it is right to threaten to do something, if you know you would never actually do it? Should you have nuclear weapons if you are not prepared to use them?

Addresses for further information on peace campaigning:

The Campaign for Nuclear Disarmament
22–24 Underwood Street
London   N1 7JG
Tel: 071-250 4010

The United Nations Association
3 Whitehall Court
London   SW1A 2EL

The Centre for Peace Studies
St Martin's College
Lancaster   LA1 3JD

New Internationalist Publications
42 Hythe Bridge Street
Oxford   OX1 2EP

European Nuclear Disarmament
227 Seven Sisters Road
London   N4

Campaign Against the Arms Trade
11 Goodwin Street
London   N4 3HQ

Jackie Pullinger

HELPING THE DRUG ADDICTS OF HONG KONG

Jackie Pullinger arrived in Hong Kong in 1966, convinced that God had called her to missionary work, but not sure exactly what she should do. She became involved in the lives of the people of the 'Walled City', a slum area famous for its violence, drugs and prostitution, and gradually came to be accepted by them. She demonstrates that, by committing themselves to Jesus and praying in his name, addicts are able to come off drugs. Now, through the work of St Stephen's Society, many of those whose lives were dominated by drugs and crime have found a new life in Jesus Christ and a new purpose, and are committed to helping others.

> **❝** *I looked around Hong Kong to see what there was to be done, and I was simply overwhelmed.* **❞**

Jackie Pullinger was born in Britain, and grew up in Croydon, South London. As a young girl she was not impressed by those who claimed to be Christians, and who wanted to convert her to their religion. They told her that she would change if she believed in Jesus. But she didn't particularly want to become like them – they seemed too formal and solemn.

> **❝** *They all looked miserable!* **❞**

This changed while she was at the Royal College of Music, studying the piano and oboe. Two friends invited her to join them in a group which met for Bible study and discussion, and she was impressed with what she found – they really looked as if they enjoyed believing in God, and they talked about Jesus as though they knew him.

> **❝** *It was then that I became a Christian.* **❞**

At a Christian meeting in Croydon, she became convinced that she should be a missionary, but she didn't know where she should go. She wrote to various Missionary Societies, but none of them seemed to want a 22-year-old music student who could teach and play the oboe and piano. In spite of this, she was determined that she should go, so in October 1966 she bought the cheapest

> **66** *I arrived with about eight pounds, but I thought I was very rich! Two things I knew: one was that God had promised to look after me; the other was that you should work wherever you can, but that you should not expect other Christians to support you. Why should they?* **99**

ticket she could find on a French steamer that was going round the world, and prayed that God would guide her and tell her where she should get off. That was how she came to find herself in Hong Kong.

Many people feel quite overwhelmed when they arrive at a place like Hong Kong. It has so many problems, so many needs. But Jackie Pullinger believes that you can see the same sort of problems elsewhere in the world – in a city like London, for example – if you really open your eyes to them. In Hong Kong they are presented in a very dramatic way.

> Where do I start?!

Hak Nam – the place of darkness

In Hak Nam, narrow alleyways run between the buildings. They are filthy and dark.

In the nineteenth century, traders from the small, British island of Hong Kong used to sell the drug opium and other goods to the Chinese who lived on the nearby mainland. On the peninsula of Kowloon (very near Hong Kong Island), the Chinese built a customs post to regulate the trade, fortified it with walls, and stationed a garrison of soldiers there. Then, in 1898, the British arranged to lease part of the mainland from the Chinese for ninety-nine years. The military base and customs post on Kowloon stayed as part of China. It became known as the 'Walled City'.

For a while it was deserted, but then the Walled City started to fill with those who wanted to escape British rule. Beyond the reach of law, it became a haven for prostitutes and drug dealers. A civil war in China led to Communist rule there in 1949, and in the 1960s there was a time of civil unrest, known as the Cultural Revolution. During both periods, the Walled City expanded to take many refugees from the rest of mainland China.

Today, the Walled City and its surrounding slums is known as Hak Nam, which means 'the place of darkness'. Narrow alleys lead down into the Walled City itself. Inside, it is dark because the houses have been built one above another, cutting out all the daylight. Although between 50,000 and 60,000 people live there, its only water supply comes from four standpipes out in the alleys. There is no proper electricity supply, and open sewers run down the alleys. Rats, large spiders and other animals share 'the place of darkness' with its human residents.

Life in the Walled City is controlled by the Triads. These are gangs of Chinese who intimidate local people, demanding protection money for their businesses, and controlling the prostitution and drug dealing. Many of the Triad members are drug addicts themselves. With no rule of law, the people of the Walled City live under the threat of violence, and because there is so much money to be made, the gangs fight among themselves for control of the opium dens and brothels.

In Hong Kong wealth and poverty are found side by side. Thousands of small boats move in and out of its harbour, and some of them may carry illegal drugs.

Modern Hong Kong consists of the original island of Hong Kong and part of the mainland – the peninsula of

Kowloon and what is called the 'New Territories', areas leased from the Chinese. Six million people are crowded into Hong Kong. It is a rich, fast-moving society. With international trade, banks and a stock market, Hong Kong is one of the financial centres of the world, and people can make large sums of money there. High-rise buildings – offices and luxury flats – crowd around the waterfront; shopping centres sell expensive goods; it is a place of bright lights and advertisements.

And yet, close to all this wealth, there are the slum areas and the homeless people, trapped in poverty and hooked on drugs. Hong Kong is a place of extremes. Every day, many people try to get to Hong Kong from mainland China. Some risk their lives doing so – hiding in goods wagons on the railway, or swimming across – attracted by the money and freedom that Hong Kong seems to offer. When they are caught, they are sent back, and some of those whom Jackie Pullinger met in the Walled City had tried many times before they were successful in getting into Hong Kong.

Making contact

Soon after arriving in Hong Kong, Jackie Pullinger was invited to help in a primary school in the Walled City! She taught the children English and music, and they escorted her to and fro, down the alleys. It was then that she started to find out what life was like for the people of 'the place of darkness'.

She would see women sitting on boxes out in the alleys, with marks on the backs of their hands where they had injected drugs. Some of the prostitutes were only twelve years old. Others were housewives who had borrowed money from the Triad gangs. If they could not repay their debts, they would be forced to work as prostitutes, and were constantly threatened with violence.

Members of the Triad gangs were very loyal to one another – and were referred to as 'brothers' – but they were ruthless in their dealings with other people.

Jackie Pullinger became a resident of Hong Kong, and she learned to speak Cantonese. On Sunday mornings, her school in the Walled City was changed into a place of Christian worship, and they held a simple service, at which she played an old harmonium.

66 *The addicts and the people guarding the dens did not take any notice of me because they were very keen on the children getting an education.* 99

66 *In a Triad society, the worst thing you can do is to betray your brother.* 99

Two years after she arrived in Hong Kong, Jackie Pullinger met an American couple, who were charismatics – that is, they believed in the Holy Spirit, that his presence and power are promised by God and available today to all Christians. As well as praying in English, they would also pray using a language that they did not understand, and which they believed was given to them by God. This is called 'speaking in tongues', and it is a supernatural gift. Jackie Pullinger had already read about charismatic worship, and when they prayed with her to receive power to make Jesus real to others, she also received a new language to help her pray. She began using this new gift to pray for people every morning.

She started to find that people were understanding and responding well to the things she was saying to them about Jesus.

Originally, she just tried to say the words 'Jesus loves you' in Cantonese, but none of the drug addicts took any notice of her. They didn't think it had anything to do with them. Then she discovered that words were not enough. You had to make real contact with people by what you did, not just by what you said.

That meant that she had to be prepared to share money, food or housing with those who were in need. She tried to help find jobs for those without work, and to visit those in prison. Gradually, over the years, people realised that she could be trusted to help them. They knew that she would visit them and accept them, no matter what they had done. She felt that it was important to accept everyone and share her life with them, because that was what Jesus himself had done.

But it was not easy. She set up a club for young people, offering them table tennis and other games – a place where they could meet away from the drugs and gambling. Before they were much older, she knew that some of them would die and others would be in prison. But the young people treated the equipment badly – they assumed that some rich church was providing it all, and felt angry because of their own poverty. One night the youth club was completely smashed up, and its walls were daubed with sewage.

She felt betrayed and rejected, but next day – in all the chaos – she went to the club again. A man came with a message from Goko (the head of the Triad which controlled the area). He had decided that the club would have his protection, and he was going to put a guard at the door

We've been watching you. Now you've been here for four years we have decided that maybe you mean what you say.

every day to make sure that there was no trouble. He recognised that she was doing something worthwhile, and that she had come to stay – she was not just going to help for a little while and then withdraw when things became difficult.

Drugs

Many of the people whom Jackie Pullinger met were addicted to drugs, especially heroin. They called one way of taking this drug 'chasing the dragon'. They would tip the white heroin powder on to a piece of silver foil, and then light a match beneath it so that the heroin melted. A little pool of heroin would run to and fro across the silver foil, and the addict would then bend over it, breathing in the fumes and chasing this dragon as it ran across the foil.

Some die as a result of taking drugs. Others have their lives ruined because they are so desperate to buy more drugs that they will do anything to get money, and therefore find themselves in all kinds of trouble. Many addicts want to give up taking the drug, but when they try to stop, they suffer many painful 'withdrawal symptoms'. Even those who go to a clinic and are successfully taken off the drug may find that, after some time – perhaps because they are unahppy, or because they mix with other drug users – they are tempted to start taking drugs again.

Hong Kong is a centre for the trade in drugs. Fishermen sometimes strap heroin to the bottom of their boats, and then sail into Hong Kong. They are tempted to do this because there is so much money to be made by selling drugs. With thousands of small vessels passing in and out of the harbour and around the 236 islands near Hong Kong, it is difficult for the police to control this kind of smuggling.

Seeing the addicts, Jackie Pullinger felt distressed that there seemed to be nothing she could do for them. But she read in the New Testament that Jesus and his disciples had the power to heal people, and that he had commanded his followers to do the same. She became convinced that the only way of getting people off their drugs was through prayer.

One of the men sent by the Triad leader Goko to guard her club was an addict. He explained that he had tried

Drug addicts lounge in an alleyway near the Walled City.

Do you want to believe in Jesus?

I'm a drug addict. How can I believe in Jesus?

If you believe in Jesus, he will give you the power to get off the drug.

If Jesus can heal me without medicine, why not?

66 *About thirteen or fourteen years after that happened, Goko himself became a Christian.* **99**

66 *We would pray with the brothers, and they would receive the gift of a new language to pray in. They think it is rather logical that God gives you words to help you talk to him.* **99**

many times to come off drugs, but each time he had started taking them again. She promised him that Jesus would change him – would give him a new life.

The man came in and started to sing, then he started praying. Without having experienced it before, he started 'speaking in tongues'. Within half an hour, he had come off drugs, and became a Christian. Goko sent someone else down to guard the club, but he became a Christian too. Then he sent someone else, and this went on for some time.

Eventually, Jackie Pullinger met Goko himself. He agreed to send her any of the 'little brothers' who wanted to come off drugs, assuming that they would returned to the Triad afterwards they would be better fighters for not being on drugs. But she insisted that, if they chose to trust Jesus and follow him, Goko should release them from their commitment to the Triad, and he agreed to do it.

Increasingly, as new addicts came in to be cured, it was the brothers who had already become Christians who prayed for them to be healed.

St Stephen's Society

Since the first 'Walled City' boy came off drugs with her in 1972, thousands have managed to do the same. But coming off drugs was only the beginning. The next stage was to find them work to do, and a new lifestyle, so that there was less reason for them to go back to drugs.

The organisation through which Jackie Pullinger works to do this is called the St Stephen's Society. Their meetings for prayer are informal. They pray for those who are on drugs, or who have been attacked and injured – singing, praying for one another and sharing the Bible. Many of those who have been on drugs, or who have lived off crime, start a new life in Hong Kong, committed to serving those who are poor, homeless or still addicted to drugs.

The St Stephen's Society has houses in which those who want to begin a new life in Jesus Christ can come off drugs and, being cared for in a family-type situation, can start to learn to care for others. Jackie Pullinger and others also visit the families of those who are in their houses, because they think it is important to help the whole family to have a new start.

In the evenings they go and speak to those who are sleeping rough out in the streets, offering them food. They take them home, where they can get a bath and a change of clothes, and they keep in regular contact with them. They try to find homes for as many people as they can. Some go to the Sisters of Charity hostel, run by Mother Teresa's nuns; others go to the Salvation Army.

Miracles

Jackie Pullinger says that a Christian is a person who having been touched by the love of God shown in Jesus, and seeing that Jesus gave his life for us, is then compelled to show that same kind of love to others, both in practical and in spiritual and miraculous ways.

She thinks that both the practical and the miraculous are important:

> 66 *If people do not show that love in a practical way to the poor and those around, then maybe they have never been touched by Jesus' love.*

> *Those who do not believe that God can intervene in life through miracles have never understood that a dead Christ was raised to life miraculously.* 99

66 *Here are twentieth-century Christians talking about miracles – well, either it's true, or they're nuts! They look at your life; and if they think that, maybe, you're not nuts, the alternative is that what you're talking about actually happens, and Christ is relevant to them.* 99

Those who are members of the St Stephen's Society do not just believe in miracles because it is part of their religion to do so – they feel that they have actually experienced miracles, in the way in which the lives of so many people have been changed.

For more information about the work of Jackie Pullinger, see her recent book *Crack in the Wall* (Hodder, 1989).

Over to you

1 Compare the Walled City with the place where you live.
   ● Make a list of the things that are different, and say how they affect your life.
   ● What feelings and needs do people have in common, wherever they live? How do you think these needs can best be satisfied?

2 Why do you think some of the young people of the Walled City treated Jackie Pullinger badly at first, but later came to accept her?

3 What do you think Jackie Pullinger meant by saying that she had to *be* Jesus for the people there? Why was that important for her work?

4 What sort of things might lead a person (not just in Hong Kong, but anywhere in the world) to want to take drugs? In what ways might these things be changed in order to help that person come off drugs, and stay off them?

Brother Roger

LISTENING TO THE YOUNG AND THE POOR

66 *Share everything that you have, and freedom will be yours.* 99

Brother Roger is the founder of the Taizé Community, in France. Through this community, he has brought together young people from every part of the world, to promote justice, peace and sharing. He believes that those who are poor are often able to celebrate together and share what they have, while the rich are too concerned to defend their own property, and miss out on many of the simple and natural joys of life. He also works for the unity of all Christians, and the community at Taizé is made up of about ninety brothers, from over twenty countries. Some are Catholics, and the others come from various Protestant backgrounds.

Brother Roger was born in France during the First World War. His father was a Protestant minister in Switzerland, and his mother was French. During that war his grandmother, who lived near the fighting in Northern France, refused to leave her home, but opened its doors to receive homeless refugees from the war. She was a Protestant Christian, but she often used to go into Catholic churches to pray, and Roger's father, although he was a minister, did the same.

Roger therefore learned from his family two important things which were to shape his life. The first was that Christian people of all different parts of the Church should come together to understand one another and to pray. The second was that he should be prepared to provide a place of hospitality and welcome for those who are in need, sharing everything with the poor.

While he was at school, Roger dreamed of being a writer and of owning a farm, but later he decided that he should go to university and study Theology. By the time he came towards the end of his studies in Switzerland, it was 1940 and France had already fallen to the German army in the Second World War. Roger decided that he should return to France to set up a house in which those who were suffering or troubled about life could gather to find new hope, where they could combine work with times of quiet, and where they could live out the Christian life.

After looking at many houses that did not seem right, Roger found himself in the town of Cluny in central France. There he saw a notice pinned to a door, about a house for sale in Taizé. He asked where that was, and discovered that it was a tiny village to the north of the town.

At that time, France was divided – the northern part was controlled by the German army, but the south was still ruled by the French. The village of Taizé was just to the south of the border between the two parts.

When Roger first occupied the house, he received a stream of refugees who were escaping south. Many of them were Jews fleeing from persecution. They often arrived exhausted, and Roger provided a place of shelter and then helped them to get away to Switzerland, where they would be safe.

An old woman showed him round the house. She begged him –

66 *Stay here with us; we are so poor, so isolated and the times are so bad!* 99

Taizé, the community which was later to promote sharing and peace between people of different countries, started during a time of war, receiving the victims of cruelty. People were making one another suffer, simply because they were from a different country or race.

Someone told the authorities what Roger was doing. On 11 November 1942, he was returning from Switzerland, where he had been raising money to help with the refugees. Before he reached Taizé, he was warned that his house had been raided by the Gestapo – the German military police. The refugees who had been hiding there were taken away; he never knew what happened to them. Roger himself escaped back to Switzerland and there continued his studies, waiting for the war to be over.

In 1944, the occupying army retreated from that part of France, and Roger, along with three friends from Switzerland (where he had been living in his family home since being forced to leave), returned to Taizé. They formed a simple religious community, living and working together.

The village of Taizé

They shared the poverty of the French people in the years following the war, and even welcomed German prisoners of war, who were allowed out of their camp to visit Roger's house at Taizé on Sundays.

Gradually the community grew. They formed a 'rule', like the earlier communities of monks, and divided their time between work, prayer and welcoming people to care for them and offer them hospitality.

Since then, the community of Taizé, led by Brother Roger, has led the way in two important things. It has brought together people from different parts of the Church – Protestants, Catholics and Orthodox Christians are all welcome to visit Taizé, and to share in its life and worship. It has also listened to what young people are saying, and has organised meetings for them to share their ideas, both at Taizé and throughout the world.

Brother Roger has described life as a pilgrimage – a religious journey. On this journey, it is the young people who are leading the way, learning to trust one another, and sharing their hopes for the future.

Bringing people together

Although they were Protestants, Roger and the first brothers at Taizé asked permission to use the little Catholic church in the village for their prayers. Very few people in that area were religious, and services had been held in it only about once every year.

The community has always tried to bring together Christians from the different parts of the Church. In 1962, Brother Roger and another brother (Max Thurian) were invited to attend the Second Vatical Council – a most important gathering of the leaders of the Catholic Church. They observed the debates that took place, and had many opportunities to discuss and share their experiences with Catholics from all over the world. In 1969, Taizé received the first Catholic to become a brother of the community. In October 1986, Pope John-Paul II visited Taizé, and was greeted by thousands of young people.

Like you, pilgrims and friends of the community, the Pope is only passing through. But one passes through Taizé as one passes close to a spring of water. The traveller stops, quenches his thirst and continues on his way.

Taizé also tries to bring people of different countries together, and to heal their wounds. In particular, the experience of war led to bitterness between people in France and Germany. As the number of visitors to Taizé increased, a new, larger church building was needed, but the community had no money for it. Then a group of German Christians, who had been working on projects in many places which had suffered during the war, came to Taizé. They donated money to help build a new church, and also sent in a team of young people to work on its construction. It was completed in 1962.

In 1971, the brothers found that the Church of the Reconciliation was too small to hold all the people who wanted to come and pray together, so they knocked down the wall at the back and attached circus tents to it.

This church is called the 'Church of the Reconciliation'. 'Reconciliation' means the bringing together of those who have been separated from one another. It was built by young volunteers from Germany.

66 *Sharing is going to mean changes in where you live. Turn your home into a place of constant welcome, a house of peace and forgiveness . . . Invite people to share a meal. A spirit of festival has more to do with simplicity than with large quantities of food.* 99

For Brother Roger and the community at Taizé, it is important that people should not be too concerned with money or buildings. What matters is the people who come to use them. Everything is 'provisional' – that means that everything can be changed in order to be used in a better way.

Brother Roger points out that it is best to live in a simple way, and to celebrate life with others. Often it is the poorest people who are most willing to share and celebrate. The rich are more likely to worry about losing their wealth, and may miss out on the more important things of life.

Bells ring out to tell people it is time for prayer. The Church of the Reconciliation is surrounded by fields of tents, where young people stay.

There are no seats in the church – everyone sits on the floor, with the brothers of the community sitting in the middle. They wear white robes.

In the services, many languages are used – so that everyone can feel that they can take part in the worship, and understand what is happening. Languages divide people from one another – it is difficult to become friends if you do not understand what the other person is saying. At Taizé, using many languages in prayer shows that all these different people have come to do something together. In their meetings, people translate what is being said into whatever languages they know, so that everyone can join in.

The common prayer, held in the Church of the Reconciliation, is at the very centre of life at Taizé. Three times a day all the work and discussion stops, and everyone makes his or her way to join the brothers in the church. Late into the evening, people stay on in the church, singing or praying silently.

Listening to young people

During the 1960s, more and more young people started to arrive at Taizé. It was a place to pray, to meet one another, and to discuss their experience of life, their hopes, and (for many of them) their Christian faith. Brother Roger was convinced that the Church needed to listen to them, for they represented the future.

Many young people arriving at Taizé have questions about the meaning and purpose of their lives. They want to know what is worthwhile for them personally. Brother Roger believes that the Christian faith can offer them guidelines, and a sense of purpose. He wants to help people to discover the 'sources of faith'. Prayer, and the discovery of Christ at the centre of people's lives, is the most important thing about the experience that people share together at Taizé.

People are helped to think about life, and to share their ideas with others. Trying to explain yourself to someone who speaks another language forces you to be simple – and sometimes that has the effect of helping you to know yourself better.

Those who have been to Taizé often join with others when they arrive back home. They form groups to continue to share what they have experienced of the Christian Gospel at Taizé.

What should I do with my life?

A discussion group at Taizé. It is an opportunity for young people from different parts of the world to meet and share their views.

In 1982, Brother Roger announced a 'pilgrimage of trust on Earth'. Brothers from Taizé had always travelled across the world, sharing the life of the poor, and this pattern was now to continue for many more young people. The intercontinental meetings of this pilgrimage take place in different parts of the world, not just at Taizé.

An icon is a special religious picture. Icons of the Cross, like the one at Taizé, have been sent all round the world. The icons are on a pilgrimage, they are passed on from one Christian community to another, and in this way travel thousands of miles. They are a sign that Taizé is not just about one particular village in France, but stands for unity and peace among people wherever they live.

Brother Roger seeks to build up trust between people, to overcome all the forces that keep people apart – to create signs of sharing – this is what the 'pilgrimage of trust' is about. As people go on the pilgrimage through life, they are called to bring peace and reconciliation to all they meet.

In 1988 Brother Roger was awarded the UNESCO Prize for Peace Education. The community at Taizé has close links with the United Nations, and ideas about how the UN can help to promote peace, drawn up by young people, are passed on to the UN through its Secretary-General.

Brother Roger spends part of every year living among the poor in the southern hemisphere. He has always taught that north and south have much to share with one another. The natural sense of happiness, festivity and fun in the south, and the greater material wealth in the north – each needs the other's help!

He questions the idea that people should be concerned about getting more and more for themselves. When he was staying in Calcutta, Brother Roger found that the people around him were desperately poor, and yet they had learned the value of sharing and friendship. He felt that the injustice in the world will not be overcome until people change their attitudes to money and power.

In 1951, when there were twelve brothers, two of them were sent to live and work in a mining area 30 miles north of Taizé. The idea was that they should share in the life of the people, especially those who were poor, acting as a sign of God's love, bringing people together to share whatever they had. Ever since then, there have been little groups of brothers from Taizé working in different parts of the world, often (for example, at present in Bangladesh) with those who live in absolute poverty.

Brother Roger himself has spent time living with poor people – from those in Calcutta and Bangladesh, to those who live in junks on the South China Sea. He has been to troubled places, like Lebanon, and to places of disaster, like Ethiopia. He has also held a meeting in Dublin, Ireland, when people from both the Catholic and Protestant communities in Northern Ireland came together to hear him. In these many different places, Brother Roger encourages young people to share with one another, and to see how much they have in common.

At the end of each year, there is a 'pilgrimage of trust' meeting in one of the major cities in Europe. The meeting lasts for four or five days, and attracts many thousands of people. The preparations for these meetings take a long time. All the Christian communities in the chosen city make arrangements so that families each agree to have one or two of the young people staying with them. In this way, those going to the meeting get to share in the ordinary life of the city, as well as taking part in the very large gatherings.

In 1974, Brother Roger was awarded the Templeton Prize, which is given to a person who has made progress in religion. He went to Windsor Castle to receive the prize from Prince Philip. The prize was given for "widening and deepening man's knowledge and love of God through his

> 66 *Resist the urge to consume – the more you buy the more you need. The accumulation of reserves, for yourself or for your children, is the beginning of injustice.* 99

worldwide work among young people, and his efforts for renewal and reconciliation".

Much has happened since then, but Brother Roger, the members of his community at Taizé, and the thousands of young people who have gathered to share their ideas and hopes, continue to *lead the way*, in seeking to live the life of Christ in their daily lives, both with those who are close by and with those who are far away.

Over to you

1 Brother Roger claims that the poor have a great deal to offer the rich, and that the people of the poor countries of the southern hemisphere have a sense of festival and an ability to share, which is often missing in wealthy countries.
   - Do you agree with this?
   - Can you think of any practical examples to illustrate it?

2 Brother Roger listens to what young people say about life, and about their hopes for the future. Some other older people might say that the young are not mature enough to be taken seriously, and that many of their ideas will change as the years pass.
   - Do you think your ideas will change as you get older? Why might this happen?
   - Do you think that Brother Roger is sensible to take the ideas of young people so seriously?

3 There have always been wars between those of different countries, or different races.
   - Do you think it will ever be possible for humankind to live together in peace?
   - In what ways do you think that the activities of Taize might contribute to understanding between people from different parts of the world?

For further information:—

A revised edition of J.L. Gonzales Balado, *The Story of Taizé* (1988) is available from Mowbray, as are many other Taizé publications:

Mowbray
28 Margaret Street
London   W1N 7LB

The *Letter from Taizé* is published every two months. It costs £4.00 for a year's subscription, and can be obtained from:

'Letter from Taizé'
Taizé Community
71250 Cluny
France

Leading the Way

VOLUME 1

Cliff Richard	Living as a Christian pop singer
Sybil Phoenix	Helping young people of all races
Jonathon Porritt	Caring for the environment
Stuart Affleck	Sharing in the life of a Christian community
Rowshon Malik	Campaigning on behalf of Asian women in Britain
Jimmy Savile	Having fun, helping people and raising money for charities
Handa Sage Shonin	Working for peace as a Buddhist monk
Cicely Saunders	Caring for those who are coming to the end of their lives
Akhandadhi das	Working to promote happiness through Krishna Consciousness
Jean Vanier	Helping those with learning difficulties

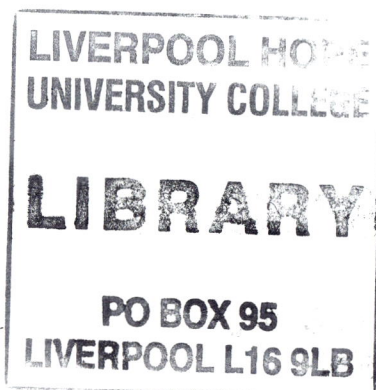